VAN MORRISON:
into the music

VAN MORRISON:

into the music

a biography by Ritchie Yorke

CHARISMA BOOKS
distributed by
FUTURA PUBLICATIONS LIMITED

First published in Great Britain in 1975

Charisma Books Ltd
37 Soho Square London W1
are distributed by
Futura Publications Ltd
49 Poland Street London W1

ISBN 0 85947 013 X

Photographs reproduced by courtesy of: Dezo Hoffmann, Trevor Humphries, Warner Brothers Records, U.K., The Northern Ireland Tourist Board and Ritchie Yorke.

Printed in Great Britain by The Anchor Press Ltd
and bound by Wm Brendon & Son Ltd
both of Tiptree, Essex

This book is dedicated to purity (an increasingly rare quantity in these declining days) and to the people around the world who, by their perception and recognition of genius shining in a garden of faded blooms and rampant weeds, have made it possible for one determined young man to create his art with next to no compromise.

The author wishes to acknowledge research assistance from articles and reviews on Van Morrison and his music appearing in the following publications: *The Berkeley Barb, Creem, Denver Post, Dublin Sunday Independent, Financial Times* (U.K.), *Fusion, Kentish Times, Let It Rock*, London *Evening Standard, Manchester Guardian, Melody Maker, New Musical Express, Playgirl, RPM Weekly, Record Mirror, Records and Recording, Rock Scene, Rolling Stone, San Francisco Chronicle, Sounds, Spotlight, The Times* of London, *Time Out, Zig Zag.*

With special gratitude to Caledonia Soul Music and Warner Brothers Music Corporation; Jonico Music, Inc; and Web IV Music Incorporated for permission to quote from Van Morrison's lyrics on appropriate occasions.

The author also would like to mention, with deep sincerity, the support and encouragement (direct and otherwise) of these fine people: Joy Annable, Alf Annable, Marcus Aurelius, Moira Bellas and Janet Fry, John Bragg, Harry Win and Kevin Carter, Judy Cooper, Ed Fletcher, Bob Gibson, Walt Grealis, Andy Gray, Ronnie Hawkins, Ian J. Hill (Manager, Public Relations, Northern Ireland Tourist Board), Ron Kass, John and Marjorie Kosh, Catharine McKnight, Drew and June Metcalf, David the Monster, George and Violet Morrison, Liam Mullan, Friedrich Nietzsche, Claude Nobs, Myles Palmer, Stephen Pillster, Juan Rodriquez, Colonel Saboo, Joseph B. Smith, Emmy Stark and Mrs Wernle, Peter and Renee Steinmetz, Tony Stratton Smith, the entire population of Wengen, Switzerland, Patrick White, and, of course, Annette, Samantha and Christie.

Not to forget for a moment the marvellous co-operation of Van Morrison, for which I am deeply grateful.

Technical assistance from Ampex blank cassette tape, Empire Electronics turntables and speakers, and Thorn/Ferguson cassette players.

Contents

Introduction

The author, yours truly etc. is truly and painfully aware that this book may not answer every conceivable question concerning Van Morrison that has flashed into your respective minds over the past few years.

The operative word I think is "every". So many myths and misconceptions have entangled themselves over the years – the media in particular appears to have all but abandoned its usual adherence to accuracy in being a source of countless unfounded rumours – that it would be a lifetime task to try and track them all down and either elucidate or eradicate their validity.

Which is not to suppose that you won't find many surprises and even the occasional revelation within these pages: indeed I believe I can confidently claim that *Into the Music* will tell you more about the real Van Morrison than anything previously published. This is not so much a boast as a matter of fact. And it is due, in no small way, to an amazing amount of earnest co-operation from Morrison himself, the man the media has so frequently claimed to be an impossible interviewee. So much for insensitive supposition.

On the desk in front of me at this moment, a rainy, noisy evening in London in July 1974, I have an article from one of the trendy fashion mags which includes a piece on Van: "Van Morrison has become a performer second only to Dylan in mystique. He is complex, withdrawn and mostly invisible. He hardly ever gives interviews and when he does, he's about as verbal as Stonehenge."

A nice squirt of metaphor. But hardly true.

Admittedly Van has sometimes acted mute in the face of inconsiderate questioning. Who's to blame him? I can only say that in the interview sessions I've conducted with him (in Toronto, London and Montreux) he has been very lucid and revealing. It is my belief that herein you will find some quite extraordinary tales of what his songs are about and where many of them are coming from. But not everything can be explained: Van frequently writes in a stream-of-consciousness style which inherently makes analysis, even by the creator, a futile endeavour. It comes as no surprise therefore to discover that even Van finds himself unable to comprehend all of the origins and catalysts in a stream-of-consciousness flow.

Which is what my opening statement was all about; not all of the questions that may come to mind are possible to answer. If the man himself cannot explain all, what hope for an outsider, he who can at best only aspire to be privy to an experience?

Into the Music then (and hopefully) is an early account of Van Morrison's first twenty-nine years on earth. Later perhaps more definitive judgments may be made.

The real nature of the man defies total penetration in the context of an interview session. He has been misquoted and misrepresented so many times that he no longer completely extends his trust to any interviewer. So many grand promises of accurate quotation were laid on him and so few proved to be true. Thus Van sometimes appears to be holding back in the confines of an interview: it all depends on the vibe he gets from the interviewer.

I must say that I was deeply honoured when I received a cable from the general manager of Van's Caledonia Productions office in San Rafael, California just before Christmas 1973, regarding a long interview we'd done together in Toronto a few weeks earlier: "he [Van] said best interview he's given . . ." Later Van told me that he'd just "felt good" that day, and "felt like opening up." It made me realize that claims of Stonehenge-like response were careless and ignorant generalizations.

When I presented a copy of the manuscript of this book to Van in Montreux, Switzerland, early in July 1974, I said to him that I did not dare claim this to be a total explanation of his music or his person, but that it was a start, an honest and accurate attempt at providing a basis for deeper understanding of his music. His life story has yet to be written. He is not yet thirty years of age, his best work is probably yet to come (even if his output thus far easily exceeds the total artistic expectations of many of his less-talented contemporaries).

Into the Music is a start; I can only hope that it serves to illuminate Van Morrison's music to its enthusiasts. It was not my intention to tell you what I think is his best work. That would be an impossibly subjective task: we all have individual and independent tastes, you will prefer one particular song and myself another. My objective herein was to make it possible for all of us to enjoy the man's monumental music to an even wider extent. His own explanations of his songs can only aid in greater understanding of his music.

A by-product of this understanding, I fervently hope, will be a broader public awareness of what the music industry is all about. You may already have suspected some of the situations which have taken place in Morrison's career as a musician, but I doubt if you will easily believe the amount of bullshit that Morrison has been put through in trying to protect and preserve the purity and integrity of his music. It's incredible that such a gifted artist has been potentially compromised by so many thoughtless music industry individuals.

I don't want to get into the assorted details in these introductory notes but I do believe that we all might marvel at Van Morrison's determination to get his music out to the public without creative cop-outs. In a merchandising-orientated industry, that is no slight aspiration or accomplishment. The more I've uncovered of his history, the more I've been amazed that he was able to survive and win so many bitter battles over the often abominable status quo in rock music.

In his eleven years in the music industry, Van Morrison has been through a hell of a lot, some of the lowest the industry can provide, and that is a considerable amount. Yet he has emerged and overcome and that is what matters. To members of the music industry who may be indignant over some of the conclusions which may be drawn from this book, I can only say that if the coat fits, wear it.

On the other hand, if this book helps to lighten the paths ahead for any aspiring young artist just entering the music industry, one would feel immense gratification. The truth and the reality is what endures in an age of horseshit, corruption and public lies even if it is so frequently invisible.

In closing this introduction, I must come right out and admit that I feel much empathy towards Van Morrison and his music. I can honestly claim that I have been deeply and profoundly moved by his art, which strikes me as being right up there with the finest contemporary music produced in these past two decades. Not only academically or technically, but in the sheer bursts of emotional response it invokes.

I doubt if I need to elaborate upon that. You too have also been deeply moved by this man's music or you wouldn't be seeking further knowledge about it. We have a common bond I believe and that's as good a note as any on which to plunge into a book.

Have a pleasant and enlightening read.

Most sincerely,
RITCHIE YORKE

July 1974

"Anything in any way beautiful derives its beauty from itself and asks nothing beyond itself. Praise is no part of it, for nothing is made worse or better by praise. This applies even to the more mundane forms of beauty: natural objects, for example, or works of art. What need has true beauty of anything further? Surely none; any more than law, or truth, or kindness, or modesty. Is any of these embellished by praise, or spoiled by censure? Does the emerald lose its beauty for lack of admiration? Does gold, or ivory or purple? A lyre or a dagger, a rosebud or a sapling?"

(These words written by Marcus Aurelius in the year 170 and included in "Meditations", originally entitled "To Himself.")

". . . . But who is in any doubt as to what I want – as to what the three requisitions are concerning which my wrath and my care and love of art made me open my mouth on this occasion?

That the stage should not become master of the arts.
That the actor should not become the corrupter of the genuine.
That music should not become an art of lying."

Friedrich Nietzsche (1879)

1 Back in Ireland looking for the *Veedon Fleece* 1973–1974

Van Morrison, footloose and worry free, arrived in Dublin with his fiancée on 20 October 1973. It had been more than seven years since his feet had last touched on Irish soil and in the meantime, his name had approached legendary status with rock fans around the world. Ireland had erupted into a vicious and deplorable religious conflict which had resulted in at least a thousand deaths with no end in sight. The Belfast Cowboy, as some called him, had produced six albums of music, four of which are among the finest achievements of rock. He had performed before hundreds of thousands of people at hundreds of concerts. To many of his fans, Van Morrison's music was hallowed, almost sacred. It provided a link to certain inner truths, to a deep sense of youthful nostalgia in a world filled with horrors of monumental proportions. And through it all flowed this gentle stream of memories of the man's own Belfast youth, as viewed from a less hostile current environment half-way around the globe in California.

He'd left Ireland for New York a mere twenty-one years old; unknown outside a hard-core minority of rock fans, his departure was overlooked or ignored by Irish media, his praises were left unsung. For the time being. He was just another disenchanted Belfast youth, aware somehow that ill was blowing on the wind, evil was grimly hanging in the air. Just another kid striking out for new spaces and places. And it's doubtful if more than a dozen of his countrymen would have had the temerity to predict that Van Morrison would return seven years later as an internationally-revered rock musician and composer; and indeed as Ireland's unquestionably greatest gift to the contemporary music world. Why even *Time* magazine, and who would dare doubt its authenticity, had named him as one of the five most important living songwriters, along with Bob Dylan, John Lennon, Paul McCartney and Leonard Cohen. And here he was, back home again in Ireland.

Although it certainly wasn't planned that way, it turned out to be an eventful homecoming. Van's original intention was just to spend two or three weeks relaxing and quietly exploring the current Irish panorama, taking stock as it were of his old stomping grounds. As one has come to expect from a man of Morrison's sensitivity, there were no TV cameras or shrewdly-planted scenes of shriekers hoarding the arrivals gate at Dublin airport. So, with none of the commotion that normally surrounds artists of his calibre, Van Morrison made what one might term a laid-back re-entry into Ireland.

He checked into a Dublin hotel, decided to hire a car and took off touring the countryside, visiting Cork, Cashel, Killarney, Arklow and even stopping by at the Blarney Stone. Van hadn't taken a real vacation in years and wandering around Ireland was his idea of getting away from the often morbid preoccupations of the North American music profession. Work was not on the agenda, not as Van had conceived it. But as it turned out, this Irish exploration provided the appropriate setting and stimulus for all of the songs on his eighth Warner Brothers album, which he subsequently gave the name of *Veedon Fleece*.

He had no plans to spend this vacation creating new tunes, but the sights and sounds he experienced and the memories they evoked, weighed heavily on his composing soul and seemed to demand instant attention. It's a well known fact that you can't just turn on this flow of artistic energy, but at the same time, the force cannot be repressed. When the spirit moves you, you've simply got to move with it. And so as Van and Carol meandered around the autumn landscapes and urban horizons of the island of his birth, a new album was conceived and one which might reasonably be assumed to be Van Morrison's dedication to Ireland.

It was a productive return in several ways. Van looked up old friends and checked out a few show bands and he even consented to make a notably rare appearance on television. He taped a special thirty-minute edition of the Dublin rock series Talk About Pop, produced by Bill Keating of Radio-Telefis Eireann. In the programme he sang several songs accompanying himself on guitar, and he also brought along Donall Corvin, an old journalist friend from Belfast, to conduct an informal interview.

Arrangements were concluded for his first homecoming concerts to take place the following spring. Just prior to his departure, Van told an Irish reporter that it had felt "good" to be back in Ireland. Admitting that it had been a creatively-productive period, he said he had written eight new songs in less than three weeks.

Van flew home to California via Toronto, where he attended the première of a film entitled *Slipstream* (in which the title song from his *Astral Weeks* album was featured) on 8 November. Already the new Irish-inspired songs were having a profound effect on his outlook. The skeletons of the tunes had taken on flesh and colour.

"I'd rather just wait until it comes out," he replied somewhat elusively to my request for elaboration on the songs. "But it is going to be more of what I'm into, put it that way. It's going to be emotionally around *Astral Weeks, Moondance, Saint Dominic's Preview* and *Hard Nose the Highway,* but really nothing like them." Yet (and I suspect significantly, since *Veedon Fleece* had yet to be recorded) he included it and *Astral Weeks* among his five all-time favourite albums.

Back in Fairfax (a community in Marin County near San Francisco, where Van lived from 1971 until the latter part of 1974), he didn't waste any time in laying down the new tunes at his home recording studio. He utilized a combination of musicians from the Caledonia Soul Express plus veteran contributors such as Jack Schroer, Jeff Labes and Nathan Rubin. When he returned to the United Kingdom in the spring of 1974, the album was completed but for a couple of minor remixes and Van was ready and willing to broaden our earlier discussions of *Veedon Fleece.*

"I haven't a clue about what the title means," was his first comment, anticipating the inevitable question. "It's actually a person's name. I have a whole set of characters in my head that I'm trying to fit into things. *Veedon Fleece* is one of them and I just suddenly started singing it in one of the songs . . . it's like a stream-of-consciousness thing."

A waiter duly sprung out from the potted palms and gleaming new décor, which recreated some other age and deposited tea and sandwiches upon our table and, as he poured, I asked Van if he'd care to elaborate on the songs.

" 'Fair Play', like all of the tunes on *Veedon Fleece*, was written while I was in Ireland last October. I have a couple of friends over there and that is a phrase they use all the time. I was just travelling around Ireland and I wrote a song from what was running through my head. So that kind of spurred the idea and it just went from there. It was just a matter of thoughts I was taking in.

" 'Linden Arden Stole the Highlights' is about an image of an Irish-American living in San Francisco. It's really a hard man type of thing.

" 'Who Was That Masked Man' is a song about what it's like when you absolutely cannot trust anybody. Not as in some paranoia, but in reality. What it's like when there's nobody you can trust at all. The guy in the song is just stuck in a house with a gun and that's it period.

" 'Streets of Arklow' comes from when we took some time going around various places in Ireland. Arklow was one of them. So I wrote a song about what I was feeling when we were there checking it out.

" 'You Don't Pull No Punches, You Don't Push the River' starts off as a love song then it goes into . . . a feeling I suppose . . . like images of things. Flashes of Ireland and other flashes on other kinds of people. I was also reading a couple of books at the time. The song has got a bit of Gestalt therapy in it too.

" 'I Wanna Comfort You' is a song about just letting somebody put the weight on you. Like when things become too much for one person to handle . . . having somebody to lean on. The end is like the reverse situation, of you leaning on them.

"*Bulbs* is definitely going to be the single. There's nothing to say about it.

"*Cul-de-sac* is just what it is. The title speaks for itself.

" 'Come Here My Love' is just a love song.

"And then 'Country Fair' is just about things that you remember happening to you when were a kid. You could say it's a bit like 'And It Stoned Me' [from the *Moondance* album]; it has the same kind of feeling anyway. It's the same kind of idea but it's not about fishing."

2 "There was no school for people like me": Growing up, schooldays, early music 1945-1963

George Ivan Morrison was born on 31 August 1945, a Virgo and the only child of George and Violet Morrison. He spent his first fifteen years in Belfast, industrial and commercial capital of Northern Ireland, sprawling around the banks of the River Lagan. By no means an ancient city by British standards, Belfast received its first charter in 1613 when it was little more than a few lanes of houses clustered around a castle. In 1816, Belfast's population numbered a mere 30,720. Then came the industrial splurge which converted so many cities into scenes of degradation and ugliness. By the turn of the century, Belfast's population had zoomed to the 350,000 mark. Today it is almost 400,000, riddled not only with the urban blight but thousands of armed religious fanatics and military occupation.

But like all industrial centres, Belfast had its upper crust which located itself as far as possible from the factories and wharves. Cypress Avenue was one such domain, a serene, tree-lined street where the above-average economic echelon escaped the ravages of industrial progress. Van Morrison grew up near Cypress Avenue and often used to wander its fanciful footpaths, avoiding the hustle and hassle of the city thoroughfares. The sympathetic atmosphere moved him deeply.

Van has described his parents as being working class: his mother had been a blues and jazz singer and his father was an ardent enthusiast of many blues singers, most notably the late Huddie "Leadbelly" Ledbetter. Born in 1885 Leadbelly led a bass" piano players who performed in Shreveport brothels and remarkable life. He was introduced to the blues by the "walking-became one of the blues genre's greatest songsters influenced in no small way by Blind Lemon Jefferson. He was thirty-three years old when he was convicted of murder, the result of a dispute over a woman, and was sentenced to a thirty-year stretch in a prison farm. Among his finest recordings are *The Library of Congress Recordings* (Elektra EKL-301/2), *Keep Your Hands*

Off Her (Verve-Folkways VLP 5011) and *Last Session Vols 1 & 2* (Folkways FP 241/2).

Leadbelly was to be one of the prime early influences in Van Morrison's career. Unlike so many of his contemporaries across the seas in England, Morrison did not stumble upon a belated discovery of the major sources of popular music in the fifties and sixties: he grew up with them. He was thoroughly aware of authentic blues and country music a full ten years before it became in vogue in London. This, one suspects, is a particularly significant factor in assessing Morrison's subsequent contributions to rock music. He had a dose of the real thing, as it were, many years before British musicians scrambled frantically to investigate what they'd missed in terms of musical education. While the English media and masses were obsessed with Tommy Steele, Cliff Richard, the Shadows, Marty Wilde and Elvis Presley, Van Morrison had been checking out the roots.

"It all started way back when I was two and a half years old," he recalls. "Ringo, my father's friend, would bring over some Hank Williams records and sit on the stairs and listen to 'Kaw-liga'. My grandfather would keep an eye on me while my mother and father were at the movies and I would make him play records over and over again. All night long, on an old His Master's Voice record player with a big horn. He dug it too.

"I'd always ask him to play Big Bill Campbell at the Grand Ole Opry I think, and one about a little red patch on the seat of some guy's pants. 'Cattle Call' and 'Texarkana Baby' by Eddy Arnold and Tex Morton, the yodelling cowboy, singing 'Big Rock Candy Mountain' and 'My Sweetheart's In Love With a Swiss Mountaineer'. What a record! Jimmie Rodgers singing 'Mother the Queen of My Heart' and whippin' that old T.B."

As the fifties dawned, George Morrison, already enamoured by American Negro and Southern white music, decided to investigate the possibilities of emigration to the U.S. "He went to Detroit," says Van, "to sort of check things out. Later he was supposed to bring the rest of the family over but it didn't work out that way. He did send me some American clothes, but the other kids were jealous of them."

Morrison feels that there was nothing unusual about his parents developing such strong emotional ties with America. Even though Belfast is by constitution part of the United Kingdom, he says it was considerably removed from the English way of life. He thinks that American influences were much stronger in Belfast because of the mass emigration to the States by so many Irish people over the past 100 years. Morrison for example had relatives then living in Detroit and Toronto and there was a constant exchange of correspondence.

Van was brought up as a member of the Jehovah's Witness faith, which possibly accounts for his commendable lack of passion about the contemporary religious horrors of Northern Ireland today. According to Stephen Pillster, a recent close business associate, Van is now "pretty a-religious". It is a subject which the man himself does not discuss.

In retrospect, his personal religion has always been music and the blues was never far from ear and mind. "My father had a collection of blues records . . . people like Muddy Waters, and Sonny Terry and Brownie McGhee. So I was hearing it constantly."

In school classrooms, Van found little to interest him. "It was really difficult for me in school," he recently observed. "The only thing I could get into was English . . . plus I was into mathematics a bit, but there was nothing much else I could get into at school. There was no school for people like me. I mean, we were freaks in the full sense of the word because either we didn't have the bread to go to the sort of school where we could sit down and do our thing, or that type of school didn't exist. Most of what was fed me really didn't help me that much later.

'When we had music classes, we'd sit and blow recorders or something. If that was a musical education, then I just wasn't impressed. I just wasn't impressed at all. That's what I couldn't figure out about that period of time – in music class they'd give you these dopey little things to play instead of just getting a record player and saying 'Like this is good and hope you dig this' or 'Here's another guy'. They had a lot of facilities that I thought they weren't using. But at home I just lapped it up. I loved classical music too."

Among the artists and styles which impressed him in early years were New Orleans jazz, folk, old Louis Prima numbers, the Woody Herman band, King Pleasure, Count Basie, even Tony Bennett, along with the omnipresent blues and country music. But Van claims that it was the aforementioned Leadbelly who "really inspired" him to start playing guitar and singing.

When he first took up guitar, it had yet to become a fashionable instrument in Ireland and Van says some people mistook it for a banjo. "I was about twelve or thirteen when I sang and played guitar. Then I stopped playing the guitar and just sang because I thought that was more important than playing guitar."

A few months later he took up the saxophone, which people considered "more hip" in those days. "I did a bit of formal training on sax for a short period of time and then I took it from there myself.

"Then I just started playing in groups . . . it was the late fifties I think. Like I had my own group for a couple of years. It was the time that skiffle was really big. It didn't matter what you played, everybody called you a skiffle group. I did that for a while and then I went on the road with a group. We had about twenty different names and none of them really meant anything."

One of the early bands in which Van played was Deanie Sands and the Javelins. Van shared the singing spotlight with the girl, Deanie Sands and also played guitar. The group played its country-blues-rock pop pourri around Belfast to a fairly enthusiastic reception.

Van was fifteen years old when he quit school in 1960 to become a professional musician, a member of a band called the Monarchs. Within a year the Monarchs took off on an extensive tour of Britain and Germany. Being under age, Van had to obtain special British Embassy permission before he was allowed to perform in foreign countries. The Monarchs appeared at many U.S. Army bases in Germany and in clubs such as the Odeon Keller in Heidelberg, the university town, and the Storyville clubs in Frankfurt and Cologne. Van summarized the era in his personal journal:

> "Heidelberg. Tram lines. The Odeon Keller, lots of good beer. My one and only movie scene. The Bahnhof. Mark Twain Village. The hotel brawl. Bratwurst. American cigarettes. Soldiers. And the music fills the room as I'm writing Miles Davis music. Big Ricky. Cognac. My surprise birthday party. Seven sets a night. Seven nights a week. Matinees Saturday and Sunday. The eagle flies on Friday. An apprenticeship they call it, paying dues. That's what it's called. It's all a busman's or woman's holiday. Right Paul Right Pete now. Waiting for the Volkswagen to come."

The Monarchs and Morrison were treated well on the whole in Germany. During one of their countless performances, a German film director was impressed by Van and gave him the part of a jazz musician in a movie he was shooting entitled *Glide*. Trivia freaks will likely be interested in the fact that as a member of the Monarchs, Van Morrison cut his first record in Germany. "It was a really bad song but we gave it a dynamite instrumental track," he recalls.

"It was the first record I played on, but not my first as a singer. I just played sax. The bass player did the singing. I only sang in the Monarchs for part of the time. I started off playing guitar then I played sax after that. I suppose I did about a quarter of the singing. I was kind of like the blues singer of the group. Two of us were really into blues but nobody in the audience was into it then. The Monarchs were kind of like a pop group with blues infiltration which nobody was really hip to at that stage of the game. So there really wasn't a lot of vocal work for me to do."

The producer called all the shots but the band desperately needed the session money. There was never enough of the stuff to go around. It was Van's first direct exposure to the inner mechanism of the record industry.

"When I started, anybody who actually thought about being a musician was considered to be a maniac, a nut or something. I remember we went for a job one time in this place in London. We were just hanging out and we'd been sleeping in the park. They didn't pay good money in those days. We'd hang out in the park and sleep there because we just didn't have the money for a hotel.

"Anyway after about two weeks of sleeping in the park, we finally got an audition for a job and when we showed up everybody in the band was wearing something different. Somebody has a brown sweater, somebody had long hair, somebody was wearing sneakers. We played about six numbers and the cat comes up and says 'You're fantastic, one of the best things that I've ever seen or heard in my whole career managing this club, but there's one thing wrong: You're a scruffy bunch of bastards and if you get some suits, you get the job.'

"So we had to get suits. There was nothing else to do in those days. Either you took it or left it. We used to play in those places where if you didn't play what they wanted to hear, you were lucky to get out alive. If you didn't do 'What'd I Say' about twenty times by the end of the set, you were lucky to leave alive."

It was during this period that Van first began composing songs. "I started doing it because it wasn't what was happening. At first I mainly wrote boy/girl things and some blues songs. But people weren't really into original material at that time. They were into copies of American rhythm 'n' blues."

And that's precisely what the Monarchs gave them. There's a glint in Van's eyes as he observes: "I was doing what I was doing when the Rolling Stones were still in school." When Van went on the road with the Monarchs in 1960, some three years before the emergence of the Beatles, the Stones and dozens of other first-generation British rock groups, their repertoire consisted of pop material as well as virtually unknown American R & B tunes by Bobby Bland, Ray Charles and Muddy Waters. In this respect they were years ahead of what became fashionable.

"We got back from Europe in 1963 and some guys were talking about opening an R & B club in Belfast. I'd been playing around and going on the road for quite a while and they knew I was into rhythm 'n' blues, more so than anybody else who was around at that time."

Yet these were still early days in the blues explosion which smothered the British music scene like an old-fashioned fog. Then (as now, incidentally) there was a sad lack of media exposure of blues or even R & B. "They were just starting to get into it," says Van. "You had to go to special jazz shops which specialized in jazz and blues records. It started to pick up around the end of 1963 and beginning of 1964 in Belfast. It was just that people who really dug that sort of music and were working in record stores would order R & B records and they didn't care less whether they sold them or not. They were just so much into that music. And that's how I got hold of the American R & B singles.

"When I'd started out playing in groups, I had Bo Diddley records when nobody knew who Bo Diddley was. That was around 1960. I used to play these records to people and they just couldn't figure them out. I used to play musicians records by Bo Diddley and Muddy Waters and they just didn't know how to react to them. And then three years later, some English group would record one of the songs and these same people would come along and say to me: 'Wow, did you hear that, what was that?' But so-and-so had recorded it so it *must* be alright. You know, a lot of the kids who came up with the Beatles don't even realize who Arthur Alexander is."

Van Morrison was different. He had always been acutely and adamantly aware of where rock music was coming from. Even if the British populace at large had been "protected" through the fifties from the alleged evils and sultry passion of such million-selling American R & B singles as Hank Ballard's "Annie Had a Baby", "Fever" by Little Willie John, Bobby Bland's "Turn On Your Lovelight", Big Mama Thornton's "Hound Dog" and thousands of others, Van Morrison made it his business to discover as much as possible of this music for himself. Since you had no chance of tuning it in on the radio in Europe, self-exposure required either an unbounded diligence in digging through the dusty bins of certain specialist record stores, or a trusting penfriend Stateside. Such hassles notwithstanding, Van thrived on his fascination with the mysteries of rhythm 'n' blues music. And perhaps the inherent difficulties of digging R & B in the U.K. during that era was an added thrill of sorts. After all any kid could turn on the radio and get into Helen Shapiro, Laurie London, Connie Francis, Adam Faith and Frankie Avalon: but it took adventure and dedication to explore the stone-walled garden of rhythm 'n' blues. As Van Morrison observed, the fruits to be found were of an infinitely finer consistency.

"When I first heard that Chicago Chess label stuff, I wanted to go to Chicago right away. I just wanted to make enough bread to go to Chicago and really hear that stuff in person," Van recalls. "Later when I did get there, it wasn't happening like that any more. I'd wanted to hear Muddy Waters live and all that stuff."

His American pilgrimage was still some years distant and in the meantime Van and the band decided to move to England for a while. "There was more work happening there. There wasn't a lot of work happening in Northern Ireland and we got tired of hassling with people who were wrecking themselves – but I guess there'll always be people wrecking themselves, no matter what."

Despite a continuing lack of money, these were pleasant days. "It was a completely different scene then. Things weren't so personal. We had a kind of show band where egos weren't involved and people weren't getting uptight over small things. I played the guitar, sax, drums; we all swapped instruments and had a good time. But in no way was it my scene up front. I was riding on the side."

It wasn't long before the band returned to Belfast where some welcome changes were taking place. A few discerning local club owners had at last detected the arrival of a fiercely-loyal minority blues cult and they began to book the well-established American blues performers who by now were making their first trips to Britain to check out the vibes and play at sporadic blues festivals. Among the artists who brought their blues to Belfast were Little Walter, John Lee Hooker, Memphis Slim, Jesse Fuller and Champion Jack Dupree. Such legendary names live on local stages filled in the gaps in Morrison's musical education to the point where he effectively understood as much about this music as almost any white youth living in New York, Chicago, New Orleans or Los Angeles.

Since he'd taken up the harmonica after hearing Sonny Boy Williamson, Van greeted the arrival of the great Chess label harp player, Little Walter, with not much less than regal reverence. He noted in his personal journal: "Little Walter was very reluctant to show me some harmonica things but that's all right because he must have been the best. He made it sound like a sax and a trumpet. Sometimes I would run errands and then he would show me something like playing a harp in several keys."

Another key influence was John Lee Hooker, who has maintained his position as one of the most talented guitar players in the blues genre. "He could play the guitar until it talks," says Van. "A lot of cats pick up the blues thing and they'd play *that* thing, but that wasn't what Hooker wanted me to play. Hooker didn't want me to play Hooker, he wanted me to play *me*. That's where a lot of people run into difficulty, because they want to cop what somebody else is doing instead of doing it in their own style. But if somebody else does something in his own style, the song becomes a vehicle for whatever style they've got in mind. That's when it's really good."

Although his pockets were rarely full of anything but harps, matches and the odd amount of small change, Morrison looks back fondly on these times. He was a student of something in which he passionately believed. In the summer of 1963, bopping around Belfast with his head full of the blues, Van Morrison was just another young Irish musician hanging off the American dream. Nineteen years old, in love with life, ladies and music, not to mention the occasional lager, he was careless and carefree. It seemed like he was on the road to freedom, whatever that might ultimately mean. But the crossroads were just around the corner and Van Morrison was about to begin a new life. His childhood was drawing to a close and he was on the verge of getting down to business.

3 Them: Meeting up with the modus operandi of the music industry 1963–1966

"The way I like to put it is that Them lived and died as a group on the stage at the Maritime Hotel in Belfast," claims *Van Morrison.*

Van Morrison has made that particular statement on sufficient occasions for the unbiased observer to assume that he means it. But with each passing year, Them appear to gain greater stature with British R & B enthusiasts, fuelled perhaps by the prevailing winds of nostalgia which are blowing up a veritable storm in the U.K. The real significance of Them would appear to be somewhat less than the rash of recent English press coverage would indicate. They seem to have more credence in 1974 than at any time when the band was actually in existence: such are the powers of hindsight. Van Morrison, Them's lead singer and focal point, is not a subscriber to the theory.

Van has frequently spoken of Them in rather derogatory terms. The band only existed for him as a performing group at Belfast's Maritime Hotel. Their music, he feels, was compromised by a deluge of uninvited outside opinion, the pressures of an industry dedicated to moulding Them into an artificial but saleable commodity. Them were seldom allowed to play their *own* music, usually they were forced to reproduce someone else's conception of what their music should be.

As a result more than a reasonable share of misconceptions has mushroomed around the real story of Them and their experiences within the music industry. "What nobody understood about that group," Morrison stated recently, "is that the whole thing was like a whole number. This was before any of the Fillmores or anything like that. But it was the same kind of vibe happening, and it was happening in Belfast. Nobody really knew what Belfast meant to Them. It didn't mean anything as far as the word didn't mean anything. It was like if that kind of thing was happening there, I think it just blew people's minds because they didn't expect it to happen that way. So that's where we kind of did our thing, the Marine Hotel in Belfast.

"We did gigs outside there too but the Maritime was like a stomping ground sort of thing. We ran the place, the whole show. Even when it came to making records, we were out of our element. Because we were there in a studio within another vibe. The way we did the numbers at the Maritime was more spontaneous, more energy, more everything, because we were feeding off the crowd. And it was never really captured on tape because there were no live recordings, or none that I know of anyway."

Them was formed late in 1963 by Van with two members of the Monarchs, his previous group, and a couple of other musician friends. The complete line-up was guitarist Billy Harrison, Alan Henderson on bass, drummer Ronnie Millings and Eric Wicksen on piano, with Van on vocals and harmonica, and on occasion, the saxophone. Soon after its formation, Them became the house band in the newly-opened R & B Club at the Maritime Hotel, playing the musical preferences of group members, essentially blues improvisation. They were good times and the memories burn brightly in the minds of Belfast kids who used to hang out at the R & B Club. Them were becoming local folk heroes. Later the R & B Club would be re-named Club Rado, providing an outlet for three prominent Irish bands in the sixties, Taste, The Cheese, and The Interns.

Them's celebrity status at the Maritime Hotel led to a recording deal being set up and the release in September 1964 of a debut single, a raunchy version of the Slim Harpo blues classic, "Don't Start Crying Now". The record was a solid Irish hit, but failed to make any impact in England where Beatlemania reigned supreme on the charts. The second single, a reworking of the traditional blues standard "Baby Please Don't Go", released in November 1964, changed everything. The intensely rhythm 'n' blues-oriented production staff of the weekly British TV pop series Ready Steady Go (one of the finest programmes of its type networked in either the U.S. or the U.K. during the past ten years) chose the single as their regular theme song. It hit the British charts in the last week of 1964 and eventually reached the no. 8 position. Them had arrived in England.

In the meantime, the group had been venturing forth on the gig circuit, playing one-nighters around Ireland with the result that they had to abandon their residency booking at the Maritime Hotel. Irish journalist Paul Charles attended one such performance in Cookstown Town Hall and writing in *City Week* magazine, detected some notable character traits developing in a band thrust into an unfamiliar environment. At the Maritime, people knew what to expect of Them, but out in the sticks it was another story.

Observed writer Charles: "Everyone was expecting one of your actual pop groups and so when Van and Them took the stage and started to play their R & B stuff, it was above most of the kids' heads, so they started to boo and yell things. This didn't go down very well with Van, so the story goes, he started to return some of the abuse which made the people very angry, to say the least. This defence of him and his group caused a near riot with the group's van being overturned, the windows of the van and the hall broken, and the group having to remain in the sanctuary of the hall until the early hours of the morning." Morrison was beginning to appreciate the price of protecting the purity of his music.

Early in 1965 Them temporarily moved to London and recorded with a prominent New York Caucasian R & B songwriter and producer, Bert Berns. The first fruit of this union, a Bert Berns-composed tune called "Here Comes the Night", was released in March. Berns had previously enjoyed heavy chart success with an original song, "Twist and Shout", a genuine rock classic as recorded by the Isley Brothers and subsequently revived, in rather mediocre fashion by the Beatles. "Here Comes the Night" was a huge hit, reaching no. 2 on the British charts and soon repeating its domestic success in the States and elsewhere. To a casual observer it would have appeared that Them were well on their way to pop's legendary fame-and-fortune status.

Irish writer and long-time friend of Van's, Donall Corvin, recalls a topical story on Them in the "Here Comes the Night" era as written by Belfastman, Chris Ryder: "Their future now is very rosy. They are quoted as earning £250 a week each, something bassman Alan Henderson denied to me. They are doing a bomb in personal appearances all over the country. In Stevenage, they doubled the average crowd when they appeared. In Bath they drew 500 more than the Beatles. In Elgin in Scotland, rag students captured them. All were mobbed and lost cufflinks, ties and even shoes. Devoted fans shower Them with presents. In the midst of all the adulation, they remain unaffected. They get angry however when they hear unkind rumours about sessionmen being used on their discs. Their image is one of moody, dirty, long-haired boys but nothing could be further from the truth. All wash regularly; their hair may be long but it's kept clean and as for being moody, well, people who say that just don't know Them!"

Morrison has been quoted on the subject of "Here Comes the Night": "It was the producer's trip, he did the arrangement and he said 'Sing this way here and that way there.' I really don't like to do the song anymore." Nonetheless "Here Comes the Night" re-appeared among his stage repertoire some eight years later, in time for the live double album, *It's Too Late to Stop Now*.

Van found himself almost instantaneously caught up in the dizzy whirl of British pop stardom; he had achieved what it seemed was the dream of every young English rock musician. Yet he was far from impressed. "I guess that we were never the same after we left the Maritime. Being on the road was just like one-night stands every night and not enough music. Too much travelling and all that stuff for next to no money. We were all just getting browned off."

Two members of the original line-up decided to pack it in. "Then, as a group, the whole thing was out of context," says Van. "The record company was trying to promote it as something it wasn't. They were inventing these images (albums jackets portrayed them as rough and ready, scruffy and scrounging, the eminently marketable angry young men as seen through the eyes of disgusted, profiteering old men). They were calling us a British group when we were really a Northern Ireland group. We were signed to London Records but we had an Irish manager: he was an Irish Jew, the worst kind, that's what they say. It was really weird. But if I hadn't been with Them, I just would have been in another band because I'd been playing in bands for five years before that, and it was no big deal for me." The two departing members meanwhile instituted a brief claim to the Them name by copyrighting it. But the laws of public usage saved the day.

Them's first album was released in the late summer of 1965. The album personnel consisted of Morrison, Billy Harrison, Alan Henderson, Eric Wicksen, Ronnie Millings plus assorted session musicians (including one Jimmy Page), hired by Decca Records against the group's wishes. Entitled simply *Them*, the album consisted of a couple of Bert Berns tunes, "Don't Look Back" (the outstanding John Lee Hooker blues number) and several Van Morrison originals, including "Mystic Eyes", "One Two Brown Eyes" and "Little Girl". *Them* reached no. 8 on the British charts, no. 1 in Ireland, no. 21 in the United States. Several hit singles emanated from this album, "One More Time" and "Mystic Eyes" which climbed to no. 29 in the U.S.).

Them's rendition of "Gloria", a Morrison original and now considered a rock classic and anthem-of-sorts, amazingly failed to gain airplay Stateside (where it was covered by an obscure studio group called the Shadows of Knight) although it fared well in Britain and the Continent. In Holland, where it reached no. 1 four times through various renditions, "Gloria" is one of the bggest-selling singles in Dutch rock history.

But as much as these singles may have impressed radio programmers and latter-day media myth-inventors, Morrison himself was far from satisfied with the finished product. In the autumn of 1973, after years of silence on the subject, Van told Roy Carr of the *New Musical Express*: "I went through a helluva lot of stuff with producers in those days, except for Bert Berns. I felt that those people who said they were producing Them didn't have a clue: between them they didn't have a solitary idea as to what we were doing. All they were concerned with was trying to push the trip on what we did. Dick Rowe of Decca Records was hanging around in the control booth when we did "Gloria" so I guess he was the producer. But that was only for that number.

"Bert Berns was the only guy who had any conception of what we were trying to do, but unfortunately he only produced a few things with us. All those other people had some weird conception of what we were about. I never quite found out what it was. We'd go into the studio and make a track and then get it played back with about ten ton of echo on it. They were all trying to make it sound like something else . . . not what it was supposed to be. Even if we'd managed to preserve what we were aiming at on the original tape, by the time it got out as a record they'd managed to mess about with it so much that it nearly always sounded like something else. It wasn't Them.

"The whole trouble was these people were locked into a stereotyped formula and they were frightened to get away from it. Once you get a tape, you can do just about anything and everything with it. That's exactly what they did. They mixed it, they re-mixed it, then took things out and put things in . . . there were so many times that it *was* happening in the studio but it was distorted on disc. There's only about two instances when the music was so powerful they couldn't stifle it. And that's why I always produce my own records now. The thing is that most producers are just frustrated artists."

There can be little doubt that Decca Records had no interest in the actual artistic aspirations of Them, and that several producers tried to shove Them into some outside image, more often than not based on what was on the top of the charts at the time . . . a typical trip being "Oh the Animals have an old folk/blues tune, 'House of the Rising Sun', at no. 1 so we'd better do a folk/blues number for a single." The feelings of the group in general and Van in particular, about Them's music was of no consequence to these all-knowing producers. "We know best what sells so just listen to us" was the directive and Them were to consider themselves fortunate that a record company was interested enough to pick up the studio bills. If the company had the necessary perception to see the potential in allowing Morrison to make his own music in *his* way, it is likely that they would have earned vastly-increased returns on their investment. But they lacked the ability and, indeed, a certain trust, and they insisted that a company-appointed producer must call all the shots. What would a bunch of doped-out musicians know about making commercial music? How could they make decisions relating to airplay acceptability? How could the group possibly know what was best for Them? Such deep frustrations to the creative spirit were to have keen influence on Morrison's widening perception of the music industry at large.

"What people in America don't understand," Van once said, "is that the music they heard [on Them albums] was not Them but session men. The *Them* album was cut by the group with session men. *Them Again* was even worse. It was me, backed by five studio musicians on four tracks. I was forced to perform under those circumstances."

It was surprising that he even bothered – until we realize that he had little choice. Van claims that the existence of an old recording agreement with Decca involving himself and bass player Alan Henderson prevented the band from completely disintegrating at this point in time. They were compelled to form a new Them to meet recording commitments, albeit this was very much against the grain. Van was obviously reaching a state of intense disenchantment with the music industry. "I was hung up with stupid contracts," he bitterly observes.

In the midst of it all, he returned home to Belfast for a change of scene. Writer/friend Donall Corvin, who was with him for much of the visit, has noted that Van "lived in a world of his own. His dreams were sweet but reality was bitter. He was a cryptic person. Gentle and quiet at the best of times but given to sudden fits of anger. His physical appearance may have given him an inferiority complex. Or maybe even a persecution complex. Whatever it was, it mustn't have been very pleasant for him." I must admit that this inferiority stuff leaves me cold. I can see no reason for it and I feel that some of the pictures in this book capture the spirit of a contemporary Beethoven figure. Van looks fine to me and if his features did wear an expression of harassment in 1965, it had to do with what he was forced to endure in trying to express his music.

He returned to Britain and played more gigs. "We were playing for a certain bunch of people," Van recalled to Roy Carr. "It was really like a cult following. It wasn't in any way a commercial trip, the thing that most groups were into of 'Let's get out and play the hits and make some easy money'. We played whatever we wanted to play, and whenever we wanted to play, and that's why it didn't work. I guess it couldn't possibly work. You can't take something like that, put it in a box and place a neat little name on it then try to sell it. That's what they tried to do. That's what killed Them."

Them Again, the second album released by Decca/Parrot in 1966, was considered by Van to be a "mish-mash" and "not really any good". His judgment may be slightly jaundiced by the circumstances, for few would argue that Them's (plus or minus session musicians) version of Bob Dylan's "It's All Over Now Baby Blue" is still the definitive recorded version of the tune. Van's "Bring 'Em On In", too, is an authentic slice of mid-sixties British R & B. Such flashes of brilliance notwithstanding, *Them Again* was marred and sorely scarred by the groping of producers towards the acceptable sound, of the Yardbirds in particular. The second Them LP lacked the purity and fire of the first album. Van contributed four original songs: "Could You Would You", "My Lonely Sad Eyes", "Bad or Good", and "Bring 'Em On In", to *Them Again*.

Shortly after its release Them flew across the Atlantic for

their first American tour, in May 1966. It was poorly organized and shabbily executed: in fact, it was little more than a fiasco. The group however made a fairly strong impression especially on the West Coast, a market hungry for any British touring talent. Them drew an enthusiastic audience reaction at Fillmore West in San Francisco. They appeared nightly for almost three weeks at the Whisky-a-Go-Go on Hollywood's Sunset Strip with two other, then-unknown, acts, Captain Beefheart, and the Doors. Frequently Them and the Doors indulged in fierce jam sessions, the two Morrisons, Van and Jim, trading off-key vocal lines of familiar rock standards such as "In the Midnight Hour". It was, say those fortunate enough to have been on the scene, a remarkable experience, a mystical combination of blue-eyed soul and black studded leather. Van and Jim shared a distinct poetic bent, something virtually unknown in rock of that time.

In other aspects, Them's Californian hiatus was not so pleasant or rewarding. The promoter who had booked them to fly to Los Angeles did a bunk with the advance money just before the group arrived. Van kept on listening and learning: it was more of the music industry experience. It was not much of a surprise to close acquaintances when, on returning to England in the late summer of 1966, Van decided to disband Them. The group had been living on bitter, borrowed time for too long. They'd had more than enough of a sick scene where integrity and honesty didn't mean a damn.

Van returned home to Belfast and found a city which no longer felt like home. Belfast was in the grip of yet another season of religious-inspired violence and hatred. Writer Donall Corvin, then a cub reporter at a daily newspaper in the city, says that within a week of coming home Van confided that he was "very confused." Corvin says: "Everybody kept telling him how big a star he was, but nobody could tell him how to make a living out of it."

Other observers have subsequently offered the proposition that Morrison's failure to cast himself in the rock star syndrome put paid to Them's success-ability, a claim which I personally find rather too simplistic. *New Musical Express* writer, Roy Carr, had concluded: "Them were the archetypal morose British R 'n' B club band: an ill-matched bunch of imageless transport-caff cowboys with clapped-out equipment who achieved some degree of immortality and notoriety in spite of their sullen selves." But Carr also claimed that Morrison had managed to "destroy the myth that you didn't have to be fab, gear or gorgeous to make good." *Time Out* magazine's Ian Hoare, in writing a 1973 overview of Van's career, observed: "Although Morrison tended to leave Jagger on the sidelines as a musician, he lacked image. Short, stocky, straggly-haired and freckled, he didn't really look the part." Which says much about the perceptive ability of the rock media and audience of that period.

Van himself is unable to comprehend the slugs of praise heaped upon the group in the post-Them period. "I don't know what it all means. I was singing just as good years ago as I'm singing now. It's very weird when you've been doing something for a long time and then suddenly somebody who didn't notice it before, notices it. But it happens with everything: everybody's like that. They may not pick up on something until years later. I do the same thing myself."

What some Them-boosters fail to grasp, I suspect, is that for Morrison, the entire Them trip was little more than a very bitter subjection to the modus operandi of the music industry. He will never feel too fond of those memories. "Them wasn't really a very happy period for me," he admitted in 1972. "Them wasn't really together management-wise. It wasn't a groovy thing and I don't consider they were good times. The good times are now."

Back in Belfast, Van found himself deeply disillusioned. People kept assuring him how talented he was but they were unable to assist him to eke out any sort of a living from his ability. All that kept him from giving up the ghost of his dream in the tensions of strife-torn Belfast were the images he'd acquired while Them were performing in California. "I'd never been to America before," he said recently. "I'd thought about going before because I knew people in the States and all that but when we did that Them tour, the days I had off gave me a chance to look around . . . mainly in California and I really dug it. I wanted to go back there.

"Somebody British saying this sounds weird, but I think America was more receptive to me . . . my type of music and where I was coming from in my head. As far as ideas and stuff were concerned, America was the place for me. That's the way it worked out. It could have been England, it could have been

Canada, but it turned out to be America. It just attracted me because people understood, for probably the first time, what I was talking about. For Belfast, my ideas were too far out. In England, I don't know whether they were too far out, or I wasn't in, or something like that. Perhaps I was ahead of my time or something."

4 Making love in the green grass with a brown skinned girl: Bang Records 1967-1968

Back home again in Belfast Van was, at least to some extent, dejected and dispirited as he approached his twenty-first birthday. He remained adamant that his true destiny lay in making music, even though he now realized that the industry which merchandised rock music totally disgusted him. Starting out as a raw recruit to the record scene with Them, he'd been the full circle of the music machine in less than three years: ripped off by gluttonous and glutinous old fools, hucksters, shucksters and all-day fuckers. The crooked bookers, agents, managers, publishers, producers, concert promoters. He'd run the gamut of the worst the music industry can offer and he found himself appalled.

Even the seemingly honest individuals, few and far between as they were (and are), invariably had no authentic rapport with the music. In the main they were crinkled old men, accountants and lawyers, "musical experts" who dealt definitively in black and white but understood very little of the grey that came between. To Van there seemed no end to it and no way around it. It was extraordinarily difficult to reconcile what this puffed-up periphery had to do with art.

Yet they quite clearly were the keepers of the keys. They opened and closed the doors that yielded or barred admittance to the pop music scene. You either made it on their questionable terms or you didn't make it at all. This hierarchy controlled the playing field; the artists and musicians were mere pawns in their game. And if you didn't abide by their rules, you might as well stay off the field. The mid-sixties was a particularly grim period in rock history. The methods of the pre-*Sgt. Pepper* era rivalled the most sinister tactics of the Hollywood movie moguls, and that says a vast amount.

In retrospect it can be seen that many recording artists not only learned to live with it, but ultimately evolved into monsters of a similar mould: scheming, money-hungry and a-moral leeches. A few feeble protests against the music establishment, a cry for the dawning of a new world, just enough time for a bitter word against the values of their parents and then into the most enormous money gorge in the dubious history of entertainment and show business. Grab the money and play their game and then back to the magnificent country estates purchased at the price of a small fortune from nineteenth-century monopolists and the like. It took real moral courage to resist the bait which the industry had set. Very few possessed it. Rather be a hypocrite than be broke.

Van Morrison failed to fit their mould. He understood the value of integrity, a substance which his contemporaries were obviously unable to comprehend. It was not at a premium, you couldn't buy a few acres of it or even a parcel of shares. It was a factor not within their frame of reference. Pity.

Morrison's dedication to his art was of higher and deeper inspiration and motivation. It couldn't be bought but it was equally difficult to sell. He'd had very few moments of comfort during Them's brief thresh in the music harvester. Bend baby bend or you ain't never gonna burn up the charts. Yet despite his overall disillusionment, he was determined to somehow see it through. If I can be excused a brief voyage upon the sea of metaphor, Van Morrison held his art before him like a lamp with which to light his way. He was grimly determined to carry it through. *They* were just another challenge to be faced and overcome.

At home with his parents in Belfast, Van contemplated his future and maintained contact with the music scene by the occasional phone call to a couple of acquaintances he considered removed from the industry's unillustrious ilk: Phil Coulter in London and Bert Berns in New York. The latter was to prove the catalyst for the most crucial decision thus far in Morrison's career.

In the early weeks of 1967 Bert Berns, an established producer and composer in the singles field, formed his own independent record company, Bang/Shout Records. In a business where track record is the beginning and the end of the holy gospel, Berns seemed assured of success. He'd co-authored the Isley Brothers' million-seller, "Twist and Shout", subsequently revived by the Beatles, the royalties from which must have topped the quarter-million dollar figure for publisher and composers. Berns had also written a tune called "Hang On Sloopy" which was recorded and achieved hit status three times with singles by the Vibrations, Little Caesar and the Consuls, and the McCoys, in that chronological order. In addition he'd produced and written a top-selling single with Them. In short Bert Berns had the wherewithal to write and produce hit singles for the AM Top 40 radio medium.

To his eternal credit (and since he is no longer around to justify his own actions) Berns must have recognized that Morrison was not yer typical run-of-the-mill British blues singer and songwriter. If it now appears that even the most unmusical type could make a favourable judgement on Morrison's amount of talent, one must bear in mind that *Astral Weeks* was still years' distant and that Berns was making his evaluation on the basis of a single recording session with Them and remnants thereof.

Accordingly Berns contacted Van and invited him to fly to New York at Bang's expense to cut four sides for release as singles. The label had already lured two prominent R & B sixties with the Goffin/King classic "Hey Girl") and Erma Franklin (sister of Aretha and herself endowed with a notably powerful delivery). The plan was for Bert to handle production on whatever original songs Van wished to record. On the surface at least, it seemed a remarkably agreeable situation.

"I had a couple of other offers but I thought this was the best one," says Van, "seeing as I wanted to come to America anyway.

"I can't remember the exact details of the deal. It wasn't really that spectacular, money-wise, I don't think. But it was pretty hard to refuse from the point of view that I really respected Bert as a producer. I'd rather have worked with Bert than some other guy with a bigger record company. From that angle, it was spectacular because Bert was somebody that I wanted to work with."

Already more than moderately enamoured by California which he'd explored on Them's first and only U.S. tour the year before, Van had by now decided that America appeared to be generally more sympathetic to what he was into. The Bang Records' offer read like a confirmation of his belief. His past relationships with Bert Berns, in the studio with Them, had been fairly reasonable in the circumstances. New York wasn't California but it was a hell of a lot closer than Belfast, even if only in a geographic sense.

"I'd wanted to go to California but I ended up in New York," says Van. "I didn't know where New York was at and I had to find out. California and New York . . . phew, it's two different worlds really. I still had it in mind to go to California, but I wanted to find out where New York was at. So I just kept California in mind until I could do it." He pauses momentarily and tugs at his unruly thatch of reddish hair.

"A lot of interesting things happened on the East Coast, a lot of good things came out of it. I really respected Bert Berns as a writer and as a musician. He was also a businessman too, like a very heavy business cat. He was into a business thing. But there's no other way you can be in New York, you're either doing business or you're not in business."

Tucking that realization into the back of his mind, Van duly arrived at the new Bang Records office in New York clutching a tape of his original songs. "Bert had a tape recorder in his office so I went up there and played the songs for him. They included tunes I was writing when I was with Them and the scene was so oppressive that I couldn't get them out, and stuff like that. So I had all this material ready to go and Bert switched on the tape recorder and said, 'Let's start going through some songs for your session.'

"The tape consisted of myself singing and playing guitar and someone banging a tambourine. We played through all the songs on the tape machine and Bert said, 'You know something, that really sounds good just by itself . . . those songs just come off by yourself like that.' But when we got into the studio it was a whole different scene: there were three guitar players, bass, drums, it was like a big production number and I felt that a lot of it was unnecessary."

At the time Bert Berns was also working on a new tune entitled "Piece of My Heart" which he wanted to record with Erma Franklin. Berns asked Van to help him finish off the song but Van, unused to working in such a manner, "couldn't come up with anything." So Berns polished the number off with the aid of Jerry Ragavoy, another Caucasian with a liberal R & B bent and himself the author of the Garnett Mimms' soul tour de force "Cry Baby". Erma Franklin recorded "Piece of My Heart" and it became a minor R & B hit. Later it was covered by the better-known Southern belle Janis Joplin (to my ear, a far inferior rendition) and topped the million mark.

Freddie Scott, too, scored first time out on the Bang label with his top ten single, "Are You Lonely For Me?" There could be no denying that Bert Berns understood the Top 40 mentality and was able to gear his material to suit its assorted artistic idiosyncrasies at the same time as pulling off extremely high calibre singles, a rare quality in those (and these) times. Singles were Bert Berns' scene and he had a knack of producing eminently marketable product.

"Bang was obviously into singles," Van agrees. "Bert was really into the singles' trip and at the start, he said, 'I want you to cut four singles.' They paid me a lot of money up front to do it. It seemed a lot of money in those days anyway, so I went in there and made four singles . . . eight songs."

The titles included "Brown Eyed Girl", "He Ain't Give You None", "T. B. Sheets", "Spanish Rose", "Ro Ro Rosey" and "Who Drove the Red Sports Car?" There was in addition a re-arrangement of the traditional blues tune "Midnight Special" and a rendition of a song Berns had originally written for Solomon Burke, the Atlantic label soul star, "Goodbye Baby (Baby Goodbye)".

"Brown Eyed Girl" (with the Sweet Inspirations singing back-up vocals) was released as a single in May 1967 and became a national top ten hit in the U.S. Critics described it as a classic journey in the summer-love syndrome and indeed it did feel to many young dudes that Van had written a personal dedication to their ladies of that summer. A lot of people discovered they were in love with a brown-eyed girl although the optical qualifications might not have been 20/20 brown.

BROWN EYED GIRL

Hey, where did we go days when the rains came,
Down in the hollow playin' a new game,
Laughin' and a-running, hey-hey skipping and a-jumping,
In the misty morning fog with our heart's a-thumpin,
And you my Brown Eyed Girl, You my Brown Eyed Girl.
Do you remember when we used to sing:
Sha-la-la-la-la-la-la-la-la-la-la-te-da,
Sha-la-la-la-la-la-la-la-la-la-la-te-da, la-te-da.

Whatever happened to Tuesday and so slow,
Going down the old mine with a transistor radio,
Standing in the sunlight laughing,

Hiding, behind a rainbow's wall,
Slipping and a-sliding all along the waterfall,
With you, my Brown Eyed Girl, You my Brown Eyed
Girl.

So hard to find my way, now that I'm all on my own,
I saw you just the other day, my, how you have grown,
Cast my memory back there, Lord,
Sometime I'm overcome thinking about,
Making love in the green grass behind the stadium,*
With you, my Brown Eyed Girl, With you, my Brown
Eyed Girl.

"They put out publicity around that time to the fact that it was written specifically about somebody I knew, but it wasn't. Originally it was called 'Brown Skinned Girl' when I wrote the song. I just thought 'Brown Eyed Girl' sounded better or something. I guess it really wouldn't have made much difference but 'Brown Skinned Girl' was the original title. After we'd recorded it, I looked at the tape box and didn't even notice that I'd changed the title. That's how spaced out it was. I looked at the box where I'd lain it down with my guitar and it said 'Brown Eyed Girl' on the tape box. It's just one of those things that happen."

Despite the success of the single, Van subsequently admitted that it had not turned out the way he personally had envisaged it. But since Berns was the producer, he felt morally obliged to go along with whatever Bert wanted. "Obviously it was a Top 40 record but I didn't think it was that well produced," Van notes.

On the chart strength of "Brown Eyed Girl", Berns urged Van to assemble a back-up group and to go on the road. The band presently consisted of Charlie Brown on guitar, bassist Eric Oxendine (later with Richie Havens) and Bob Grenier on drums. "I got to play in some wrong places," says Van. "That's

* (Some radio stations, incredibly, took it upon themselves to censor this line).

one thing the single hit did: it put me in some of the worst joints I ever worked. I don't want to mention any names or offend anybody in the business but it put me in some awkward positions because the places were unreal. They were totally unreal."

With the three-quarters of a million sales on "Brown Eyed Girl" and the release of "Ro Ro Rosey" as the follow-up, Bang decided to issue its first Van Morrison solo album *Blowin' Your Mind*. All proceeded according to company schedule, but somehow Bert Berns neglected to inform his artist of the plans. "I got a call from a friend one day," says Van, "and this guy says, 'Hey I got your album, man.' And I said, 'What album?' Bang had turned around and put out an album of these four singles and I didn't even know about it! The first album on Bang wasn't even an album. We hadn't even gotten around to discussing that album when they put it out. It was only eight cuts for four singles."

Writer Danny Holloway, upon concluding that *Blowin' Your Mind* was produced amid a lot of artistic frustration, was told by Morrison: "I don't think that album really had anything to do with where I was at. An album is just an album. You do it when you're doing an album, and then after you've done it, it's done. It may reflect where you were at in one given period of time but after you've done the album, it's over. My life can't revolve around an album. I mean it's just an album. An album is roughly forty minutes of music, that's all."

More than slightly pissed off at this point in time, Van decided to move away from the New York scene to Cambridge near Boston. The Big Apple wasn't bringing much joy to his creative soul. "Cambridge was very funky," he recalls. "It's a college town and there are a lot of funky clubs and a lot of bars when you can see R & B performers. I don't think it had any effect on my music or anything like that but I liked Cambridge."

Several months thus passed, but eventually a persistent Bert Berns persuaded Morrison to take a crack at some more studio sessions. Van was to be allowed to make his own album. "The second album for Bang was supposed to be *my* album" says Van, a trifle bitterly. "After I'd had a run in with Bert about that first album, he said, 'Well you make the second one and you do whatever you want to do,' but he didn't let me do what I wanted to do.

" 'O.K.,' I said, 'Give me a shot at what I want to do.' But he still didn't let me do what I wanted to do. When it came time for the sessions, there was about a ten-piece rhythm section and out of that, five people we didn't need. The engineer just didn't seem to care about the sessions at all. And I didn't have my chance at 'my shot' as Bert put it."

Nonetheless Bang's second Morrison album, *The Best of Van Morrison*, was released in the latter months of 1967. It too could hardly be called a fair representation of what the man was trying to achieve. It included five cuts from the *Blowin' Your Mind* LP plus five new Morrison songs: "It's All Right", "Send Your Mind", "The Smile You Smile", "The Back Room", and "Joe Harper Saturday Morning". One of the newer tracks not used for this album, it's worth mentioning, was a strenuous, stream-of-consciousness number called "Madame George". Later it would be dug out of the vaults by Bang for inclusion on an unauthorized album.

Morrison undoubtedly was still at the mercy of outside influences in the making of his music yet his involvement with Bang Records, for all of the obvious frustration, was still an improvement on the Them situation. Progress was being made, slow and tedious though it might be. Things of course could have been better but they also could have been much, much worse by the yardsticks of the music industry.

But as fate would have it, Van had little time in which to speculate on such progress. Bert Berns and Van Morrison had completed their last recording sessions together. On 1 December 1967, Berns succumbed to a fatal heart attack which stunned the music industry and ended Van's association. "Bert was really a nice guy," Van concluded not long ago. "It was really weird when he died. Like one day he was in the office, I remember seeing him there, and then the next day he was dead."

5 "*Astral Weeks* was to have been multiple sketches upon a visually-orientated concept": *Astral Weeks* 1968

"Genius" observed Owen Meredith, the Earl of Lytton, in the nineteenth century, "does what it must, and Talent does what it can." Such perceptive and poetic words strike one as an appropriate way in which to begin the exploration of *Astral Weeks*, unquestionably one of the very few genuine masterpieces of popular music. On the unique, unbending strength of this album alone, Van Morrison deserves consideration as a musical genius.

One does not of course make such a statement lightly, nor without lengthy contemplation of our collective artistic heritage. And in arriving at this conclusion (which by no means is either new or over indulgent) I am taking into account the amazing circumstances which surrounded the production of *Astral Weeks*, to be dealt with here in due course.

For all of the music industry's often hysterical hyperbole, genius has not been a frequent attender upon the rock scene. Practically anyone has the necessary inherent ability to become a guitar player, and you don't need any staggering gift to churn out a 150-second pop song. Needless to say there are varying degrees of expertise, but the fact remains that you and I could attain a passable standard of performance on the six-string electric guitar within a mere half-year of first picking up the instrument. Plenty of hits have been recorded by rock musicians with less than six months' experience. It's all relative: it takes years to acquire reasonable prowess on the violin for example, while learning the rudiments of the guitar involves mere months.

Not for a moment am I endeavouring to undermine the emotional pleasure of hearing a guitar well played, but I do believe it's relevant to present an opinion that the instrument is eminently accessible to large numbers of people. Which could well be its most significant attribute. Practically anyone can play it. And some of the best-known rock guitarists in the world will never be accused of being intellectual heavyweights. Less generous observers might well point out that a few of them are more than a bit thick. It all depends on what yardstick you're applying.

One is inclined to doubt that even a fervent fan would make a sober claim that Elvis Presley, for instance, is a genius. He may be a damn good rock 'n' roll singer and a hell of a robust entertainer, but he ain't no genius. I suppose that collectively the Beatles exhibited flashes of genius but I would never use the term to describe any one of the four individuals. Others have tried to pin the crown on Chuck Berry and I'm ready to admit that no single individual in the world of music captured the spirit and feeling of the fifties with so much verve and authenticity. Ray Charles too has been singled out on many occasions as a musical genius. The word has often been utilized to summarize the considerable talents of one Bob Dylan.

It has been used with notorious looseness too, on sufficient individuals to take the real bite and sting out of the true significance of the word. If one were to believe what the music publicists are continually claiming, the record industry has enough genii to over-populate Manhattan Island.

Perhaps by traditional terms, rock music has not produced a single genius of the calibre of a Beethoven or a Mozart. But these two masters gave their whole lives to posterity, only a handful of rock artists have now completed their artistic work (for whatever reason) and their finest moments may be yet to come. Nevertheless, if ever any popular music artist of the past two decades warranted serious consideration for such an accolade, I firmly believe it is Van Morrison. My pocket Collins Dictionary protrays a genius thus: "highest mental ability; one with this natural bent or inclination of the mind, tutelary spirit, character, spirit." I remain adamant: Van Morrison fills the bill.

Similarly it is exceedingly difficult to think of any piece of music produced in these last twenty years (or indeed at any time in this century) which has had such a profound effect on its audience as *Astral Weeks*. Individual responses to the magic of this musical album are of sufficient quantity and fervour to fill an entire volume and I would heartily recommend the project to prospective authors and publishers. It could well put us much further along the road to understanding how and why this music has become such an unprecedented universal phenomenon, easily eclipsing in sheer market bulk any other artistic medium active since World War II.

The reaction to *Astral Weeks* transcends language and class barriers and has deeply moved people, it would seem, in all corners of the earth. I have personally heard the album praised and contemplated in reverent tones in such far removed centres as Rio de Janeiro, Sydney, Tokyo, Vancouver, London, Madrid, the Swiss Alps and all over North America. Yet the geographical spread is only barely significant when compared with the depth and colour of emotion which the album arouses in its listeners. It really does reach across that void which separates the artist stamped into a piece of black plastic and his audience, and it transforms the relationship into something quite remarkable. It completely dominates one's soul. It achieves a unique juxtaposition with one's emotions. It seems in harmony with one's flow of life.

That *Astral Weeks* could achieve such one-to-one communication in the early months after its release is astounding enough; that it should continue to kindle the flames of passion a full six years after its birth is, I think, something of pure magic. All sorts of absurd reasons have been dragged forth to account for this exceptional quality. One of the more fashionable was that the album's arrival coincided with the heady peaks of the post-Pepper dope era. I must say that I find such rationale altogether too simplistic. I suspect that there is much, much more to the *Astral Weeks* situation than the undoubted special pleasure of listening to it with a few tokes under the belt. Which is not to imply that this album does not benefit, as do all albums, from the depth of attention span accorded it by its listener.

Analysing the musical qualities of *Astral Weeks* is a precarious task, all the more so because no album in rock history has been so thoroughly difficult to categorize. It simply does not fit neatly into any accepted pigeonhole or genre. It is not a blues record even though the blues influences are quite apparent. It is clearly not a folk album either, despite the stunningly-sensitive interplay of acoustic instruments. There are tinges of jazz in some of the tunes and especially through the use of upright bass, but in the main the rhythm section is propelled with a rock vision. The vocals too are of such diversity that one trite little collection of terminology would be entirely unsatisfactory.

All told one is inclined towards the viewpoint that *Astral Weeks* is an album of music, free from adjectival intrusion. It is simply music of an infinitely tender expression, unable to be labelled because it is – despite obvious eclecticism – the first and only of its kind. It sets precedents rather than follows them. It was almost as if Van Morrison, elusive at any time, had deliberately created an album of music which would indefinitely withstand the vulgarity of music industry image-making. Later they might say that other albums were reminiscent of *Astral Weeks*, but they could never claim that *Astral Weeks* was like anything else. They wouldn't be able to pin down either the man or his music. They couldn't call it folk/rock or white blues or heavy metal or any of the other categories into which rock music fitted, it was only Van Morrison's music.

That's the way Morrison likes things to be and who could fairly blame him? Anything else is subjective opinion and, to Morrison's mind, product-oriented which in his view is the capital sin. And so, to gain any further insight into *Astral Weeks*, the ideal method of investigation is to look into the words of Van Morrison himself.

In the early summer of 1968, Van Morrison was working the east coast of America for not much more than union scale, fronting a trio which consisted of flautist John Payne (who now works in Cambridge, Mass. with singer/songwriter Peter Johnson and his brother Hunter Payne, and can also be heard on Andy Pratt's debut album for CBS), Tom Kilbania on upright bass, with Van handling vocals. One is tempted to feel that it was an unlikely combination, certainly in an instrumental sense.

"The regular band was three pieces and it was really weird because only afterwards did people realize what we were doing," Van claimed recently. "People may recognize it now, but then they didn't have a clue. We used to play clubs and people like Jimi Hendrix would come up and sit right in front and listen all night. I don't know . . . it seemed the musicians dug it but the general public didn't know what we were into."

One person who did seem to have some degree of appreciation of Morrison's potential at the time was Joseph B. Smith, a former disc jockey who had worked his way up to be president of Warner Brothers Records. In the early stages of this relationship, Smith felt that Morrison had strong potential as a singles artist. "You must remember," Smith told me not long ago, "that single records were much more of a factor in establishing artists at that time than they are now. Van had a history of being around the pop single feeling and charts and that was of great interest to us."

Morrison makes no secret of the fact that he had been contemplating signing with Warner Brothers for a considerable period of time before the union actually took place. "I'd been talking to Warner Brothers for years," he says, "even when I was with Bang. Warner Brothers were romancing me even then. So it wasn't anything new for me. It just took a couple of years to get together. It wasn't any snap decision . . . I'd been thinking about it for years."

Adds Joe Smith: "A guy called Andy Wickham was valuable in setting up the first contacts for Warner Brothers and I followed up after that. I seem to remember about six months of contacting and attempting to negotiate out of his previous deal and the straightening out of his immigration status before we could proceed with the signing."

With names signed on the papers, plans were set up for Van's first recording sessions for the new label. The songs he wanted to try out were most definitely not of overnight vintage: the entire album in fact had been carefully contemplated for many months. "Most of the songs were written about six months before the album was recorded. I was playing most of the tunes for a while before we did the album." Unlike many highly-regarded rock albums, *Astral Weeks* was not cranked out while groping in the studio; Van had very clear-cut ideas on its shape and form; never before had he been so sure of exactly what he wanted to do with an album.

"*Astral Weeks* was a whole concept from beginning to end," he says flatly. "It was all thought out up front. Originally it was supposed to be an opera. By opera, I mean multiple visual sketches. When I had written the songs, there was talk of a film. So it was a visually-oriented concept. The producer wanted to do a film of it and we tossed that idea around for a while but it didn't really happen."

Much speculation has been written around the alleged fact that *Astral Weeks* represented Morrison's first measure of artistic control of his work. No less an authority than *Rolling Stone* claimed, in a lengthy Morrison profile of June 1972, that *Astral Weeks* allowed him: "artistic control for the first time in his career." This is only partly true. Nobody would deny, firstly that Van's two albums for Bang and his work with Them allowed him little artistic self-expression. They were all produced by an outside party, who had the final decision on all matters. Morrison considered himself fortunate if he was allowed to select song repertoire, which is a fairly grim state of affairs.

Astral Weeks was a step in an improved direction, but there is no shortage of proof that true artistic freedom was still several albums distant. Morrison did not have artistic control of *Astral Weeks* albeit he did have more creative involvement than in any previous album.

According to the official credits, *Astral Weeks* was produced by Lewis Merenstein of Schwaid/Merenstein Productions through which Morrison's Warner Brothers contract had been negotiated. "I was signed for one year with an independent production company," says Van, "and not directly to Warner Brothers. So I didn't have the freedom to say what tracks would come out."

In his wisdom, Merenstein, who was calling the shots, came to the conclusion that only one of Van's two regular backing musicians was of the necessary calibre to participate in the recording of *Astral Weeks*. "The producer was sort of controlling the sessions," Van notes, "and so the flute player John Payne plays on a lot of the tracks but the bass player wasn't used." In August 1973, Van told *ZigZag* magazine editor, John Tobler that it *could* be said that he personally produced *Astral Weeks* since: "it all depends on what you mean by producing . . . Merenstein was a kind of executive producer, an ex-engineer."

There is no shortage of astounding circumstances surrounding the *Astral Weeks* album, but I am convinced that none more so than the virtually unbelievable fact that the entire LP was recorded in: "two eight-hour sessions, plus two overdub sessions. That was the whole album." Perhaps Van's words require a degree of dissection for the layman. These days, a big group which recorded one single in comparative time would consider itself working too fast. The average album in the mid-seventies takes several hundred hours to put together; a few have broken into four-figure hour totals. Many musicians labour under an unsupportable myth that the longer the time spent in the studio, the better the product. It may be true in some individual cases, but as a working rule it is just not valid. If *Astral Weeks*, surely the equal of almost any album ever recorded during the past couple of decades, could be produced completely in four sessions then it rates even more abundant acclaim.

You will understand that in the brief few hours devoted to the recording of *Astral Weeks*, there was very little messing around. "The whole album was recorded live," says Van. "The only overdubbing of instruments were the strings and a couple of horns in two numbers. The songs came together very well in the studio. Some of the tracks were first takes. The musicians (Jay Berliner on guitar, bassist Richard Davis, Connie Kay of the Modern Jazz Quartet on drums, and Warren Smith Jr. on percussion and vibes, plus flautist John Payne) were really together. Those type of guys play what you're gonna do before you do it, that's how good they are."

Even though Van has on occasion expressed the opinon that the album was "rather rushed", he said very recently that he was: "happy with the whole album. It just stands out."

Consider also that in addition to the eight songs you hear on your copy of *Astral Weeks*, the two sessions produced two other tracks plus rumours of a strange forty-five minute song which has been the subject of a good deal of speculation.

"It's not true that we recorded a forty-five minute track for *Astral Weeks*," says Van. "The truth is that I had a song at that time that was about forty-five minutes long, but it wasn't recorded for the album. I don't think that I could ever do it again. I made a rough tape recording of it with just myself and another guitar player and we sat down and I did it onto a small tape. But I didn't try it again because I knew that I couldn't recapture what we had before. The original tape was just so spontaneous. Even the lyrics were spontaneous. I could sing them again, but I could never sing them the same way. So I never tried.

"There were only two tracks we recorded that did not appear on *Astral Weeks*. One was about Jesse James and the other about trains. They were both just basic blues numbers. That's why they didn't fit in with the album. They were both in another bag. The trouble is that you can never get everything on an album. It's very hard to do your number in forty minutes so you always have stuff in the can."

The eight songs ultimately selected by Merenstein for inclusion on *Astral Weeks* were divided into two separate sections: In The Beginning included the title song, "Beside You", "Sweet Thing", and "Cypress Avenue", while Afterwards featured "The Way Young Lovers Do", "Madame George", "Ballerina" and "Slim Slow Slider". An awful lot of nonsense has been written about what each song secretly represents, but as Van himself slyly observes: "It's all in *your* head." The subjective viewpoint is once again in the spotlight and one man's meat will always be another's poison.

There is reason to believe, I think, that Van's personal impressions of the songs, recently expounded on for the first time, tell us more about *Astral Weeks* than any previous critical surmisals or appraisals.

ASTRAL WEEKS

If I ventured in the slipstream between the viaducts of
  your dreams,
Where immobile steel rims crack, and the ditch in the
  back roads stop,
Could you find me, would you kiss-a my eyes,
And lay me down in silence easy, to be born again, to be
  born again.

From the far side of the ocean if I put the wheels in
  motion,
And I stand with my arms behind me and I pushed
  another door,
Could you find me, would you kiss-a my eyes,
And lay me down in silence easy, to be born again, to be
  born again.

There you go standing with the look of avarice,
A-talkin' to Huddie Leadbelly a-showing pictures on the
  wall,
A-whispering in the halls and pointing a finger at me,
There you go there you go standing in the sun darlin',
With your arms behind you and your eyes before,
Well, there you go, taking a care of your boy,
A-seeing that he's got clean clothes,
A-putting on his little red shoes,
A-pointing a finger at me.
And here I am, standing in your sad arrest, trying to do my
  very best,

Looking straight at you, and coming through, darlin',
To be born again, to be born again,
To be born again, in another world darlin'.
In another world,
In another time,
Got a home on high.
Ain't nothin' but a stranger in this world,
I'm nothin' but a stranger in this world,
I got a home on high,
In another land so far away, so far away.
Way up in the heaven,
Way up in the heaven,
Way up in the heaven,
Way up in heaven.
In another time,
In another place,
In another time,
In another place,
And another face.

"*Astral Weeks* is like a transformation song," Van explains. "It's like transforming energy, or going from one source to another with it being born again like a rebirth. I remember reading something somebody said about you having to die to be born. It's kind of one of those songs where you can see the light at the end of the tunnel and that's basically what the song says. I don't think I can elaborate on it any more than that."

It should be mentioned at this point that this track was used some five years later as the title song in a Canadian-made film named *Slipstream*. "The film was directed by a Canadian guy called David Acomba," Van says. "It won the National Film Board of Canada award and it has been banned in a lot of places. It was banned because it exposes a lot of the corruption in the music business. It's about a disc jockey who is straight and anti-commercial and his boss wants him to get an image. He won't conform so they destroy him. I think it's a great film. And I think that 'Astral Weeks' is in context with the film . . . I think it works really well. The subject has been taboo for a long time and it's about time that it got out into the light. It's just the whole commercial scene."

BESIDE YOU

Little Jimmy's gone way out of the back street,
Out of the window, to the fog and rain,
Right on time, right on time.
That's why Broken Arrow waved his finger down the road so dark and narrow,
In the evening just before the Sunday six-bells chime, six-bells chime,
And all the dogs are barkin',
Way out on the diamond studded highway where you wander,
And you roam from your retreat and view,
Way over on the railroad,
Tomorrow all the tipping trucks will unload together,
Ev'ry scrapbook stuck with glue,
And I'll stand Beside You,
Beside You Oh child,
To never, never, never wonder why at all,
No, no, no, no, no, no, no, no,
To never, never wonder why at all,
To never never never wonder why, it's gotta be,
Oh darlin',
To never never wonder why at all,
No, no, no, no, no,
To never, never, never wonder why at all,
To never, never, never wonder why, it's gotta be,
It has to be, and I'm Beside You,
Beside You, oh child,
To never, never wonder why at all,
I'm Beside You, Beside You, Beside You,
Oh child.

It has to be 'way across the country where the hillside mountains glide,
The dynamo of your smile caressed the barefoot virgin child to wander,

Past your window with the lantern lit.
You held it in the doorway,
You kissed against the pointed idle breeze,
And said your time is open, go well on your merry way,
Past the brazen footlights of the silence easy.
You breathe in, you breathe in, you breathe in, you breathe in,
And you're high on your flying cloud,
Wrapped up in your magic shroud as ecstasy surrounds you,
This time it's found you,
You turn around, you turn around, you turn around, you turn around,
And I'm Beside You, Beside You.

"Beside You," says Van "is the kind of song that you'd sing to a kid or somebody that you love. It's basically a love song. It's just a song about being spiritually beside somebody."

SWEET THING

And I shall stroll the merry way and jump the hedges first,
And I will drink the clear, clean water for to quench my thirst.
And I shall watch the ferry boats and they'll get high.
On a bluer ocean against tomorrow's sky,
And I will never grow so old again.
And I will walk and talk in gardens all wet with rain,
Oh, Sweet Thing, Sweet Thing,
My, my, my, my, my Sweet Thing.

And I shall drive my chariot down your streets a-cryin',
'Hey it's me, I'm dynamite, and I don't know why,'
And you shall take me strongly in your arms again,
And I will not remember that I ever felt the pain.
We shall walk and talk in gardens all misty wet, misty wet,
And I will never, never, never grow so old again.

And I will raise my hand up into the night time sky,
And count the stars that's shining in your eye,
Just to dig it all and not to wonder, that's just fine,
And I'll be satisfied not to read between the lines.
And I will walk and talk in gardens all wet with rain, with
rain,
And I will never, ever, ever, ever grow so old again.

" 'Sweet Thing' is another romantic song. It contemplates gardens and things like that . . . wet with rain. It's a romantic love ballad not about anybody in particular but about a feeling."

CYPRESS AVENUE

I'm caught one more time up on Cypress Avenue,
Caught one more time on the Cypress Avenue,
I'm conquered in a car seat,
Not a thing that I can do.
I may go crazy before that mansion on the hill,
I may go crazy before that mansion on the hill,
But my heart keeps beating faster,
And my feet can't keep still.
And all the little girls rhyme something,
On their way back home from school,
And all the little girls rhyme something,
On their way back home from school,
And the leaves fall one by one,
And call the Autumn time a fool.

And my tongue gets tied,
Every, every, every time I try to speak,
My tongue gets tied every time I try to speak,
And my insides shake just like a leaf on a tree.
But I think I'll go walk by the railroad with my cherry,
cherry wine,
I believe I'll go walking by the railroad with my cherry,
cherry wine,

But if I pass the rumblin' station,
Where the lonesome engine drivers pine.

Yonder comes my lady,
Rainbow ribbons in her hair,
Yonder comes my lady,
Rainbow ribbons in her hair,
Six white horses on a carriage,
Just returning from the Fair.
Way up on, way up on, way up on,
The avenue of trees,
You came walkin' down, in the wind and rain darlin',
When you came walkin' down the sun shone through the trees,
And nobody . . . can stop me from loving you baby,
So young and bold,
You're fourteen years old.

" 'Cypress Avenue' is a street in Belfast," says Van, "a place where there's a lot of wealth. There are a lot of areas in Belfast where there was a lot of wealth and 'Cypress Avenue' is one of them. It wasn't far from where I was brought up and it was a very different scene, financially or whatever you might want to call it. To me it was a very mystical place. It was a whole avenue lined with trees and I found it a place where I could think. Instead of walking down a road and being hassled by forty million people, you could walk down Cypress Avenue and there was nobody there. It wasn't a thoroughfare. It was quiet and I used to think about things there."

THE WAY YOUNG LOVERS DO

We strolled through fields all wet with rain,
And back along the lane again,
There in the sunshine, in the sweet summer time,
The Way that Young Lovers Do.

I kissed you on the lips once more,
And we said goodbye at your front door,
In the night time, Yeah that's the right time,
To find The Way that Young Lovers Do.
Then we sat on our own star and dreamed of the way that
we were and the way that we wanted to be.
Then we sat on our own star and dreamed of the way that
I was for you and you were for me.
And then we danced the night away,
And turning to each other say,
"I love you, I love you,"
The Way that Young Lovers Do.

"On the second side," continues Van, " 'Young Lovers Do' is just basically a song about young love." And he laughs mysteriously.

MADAME GEORGE

Down the Cypress Avenue,
With a child-like vision leaping into view,
The clicking clacking of the high-heeled shoes,
Ford and Fitzroy, Madame George.
Marching with the soldier boy behind,
He's much older now with hat on, drinking wine,
And that smell of sweet perfume comes drifting through,
In the cool air like shalimar.
And outside they're making all the stops,
The kids out in the streets collecting bottle tops,
Going for cigarettes and matches in the shops,
Happy taking Madame George,
And that's when you fall,
Oh Oh that's when you fall,
Yeah that's when you fall.

And you fall into a trance,
Sitting on a sofa playing games of chance,

With your folded arms in history books you glance,
Into the eyes of Madame George.
And you think you've found your bag,
You're getting weaker and your knees begin to sag,
And in the corner playing dominoes in drag,
The one and only Madame George.
And from outside the frosty window raps,
She jumps up and says "Lord have mercy,
I think that it's the cops",
And immediately drops everything she gots,
Down into the street below.
Now you know you gotta go,
On a train from Dublin up to Sandy Row,
Throwing pennies at the bridges down below,
In the rain, hail, sleet and snow.

Say goodbye to Madame George,
Dry your eyes for Madame George,
Wonder why for Madame George,
Wonder why for Madame George.
And as you leave the room is filled with music,
Laughing music, dancing music all around the room,
And all the little boys comin' round,
Walking away from it all, so cool.
And as you're about to leave she jumps up,
And says "Hey love, you forgot your glove",
And the love that loves the love that loves the love that
loves,
The love that loves to love the love that loves to love the
love that loves,
Say goodbye to Madame George,
Dry your eyes for Madame George,
Wonder why for Madame George,
Dry your eyes for Madame George.

" 'Madame George' was recorded live," says Van. "The vocal *was* live and the rhythm section and the flute too and the strings were the only overdub. The title of the song confuses one, I must say that. The original title was Madame Joy but the way I wrote it down was 'Madame George'. Don't ask me why I do this because I just don't know. The song is just a stream-of-consciousness thing, as is 'Cypress Avenue'. Both those songs just came right out. I didn't even think about what I was writing. There are some things that you write that just come out all at once, and there's other things that you think about and consider where you'll put each bit.

" 'Madame George' just came right out. The song is basically about a spiritual feeling. It may have something to do with my great aunt whose name was Joy. Apparently she was clairvoyant . . . that may have something to do with it. Aunt Joy lived around the area I mentioned in connection with Cypress Avenue. She lived in a street just off Fitzroy Street which is quite near to Cypress Avenue."

Morrison's fiancée suspects the song also might have something to do with Van's father, George. Van simply shrugs at the suggestion. He really knows no more.

BALLERINA

Spread your wings, come on, fly awhile,
Straight to my arms oh, little angel child,
You know you're only lonely twenty two story, bla.
And if somebody not just anybody,
Wanted to get close to you,
For instance, me, baby,
All you gotta do is ring the bell,
Step right up, step right up,
Step right up, Ballerina.

Grab it, catch it, fly it, sigh it, try it,
Well, I may be wrong,
But something deep in my heart tells me,
I'm right and I don't think so.
You know I saw the writing on the wall,
When you came up to me,
Child, you were heading for a fall.
But if it gets to you,
And you feel like you just can't go on,
All you gotta do is ring the bell,

Step right up, step right up,
Step right up, just like a Ballerina,

Stepping lightly,
Grab it, catch it, fly it, sigh it, die it.

Well, it's getting late, yes it is, yes it is,
And this time I think you should slip into your slumber,
The light is on the left side of your head,
And I'm standing in your doorway and I'm mumbling,
And I can't remember the last time you ran through my head,
Here comes the man, here comes the man,
And he says, he says the show must go on.
All you gotta do is ring the bell,
Step right up, step right up,
Step right up, just like a Ballerina.

Grab it, catch it, fly it, sigh it, die it,
Just like a Ballerina,
Just like a Ballerina,
Get on up, get on up,
Keep a movin' on up, just a little higher, baby,
Get on, get on,
Keep on, keep on pushin', keep on pushin', keep on pushin'.
Steppin' lightly,
Just like a Ballerina,
Take off your shoes,
Just like a Ballerina.

" 'Ballerina'," Van admits, "is one track that I really don't know much about. I had a romantic image in my head about the San Francisco outlook. I think that's where the song comes from. I was in San Francisco one time in 1966 and I was attracted to the city. It was the first time I'd been there and I was sitting in this hotel and all these things were going through my head and I had a flash about an actress in an opera house appearing in a ballet and I think that's where the song came from. The song may possibly be about a hooker. Part of it anyway may be about a hooker, but other than that, it's just poetry."

SLIM SLOW SLIDER

Slim Slow Slider, horse you ride is white as snow,
Slim Slow Slider, horse you ride is white as snow,
Tell it everywhere you go.
Saw you walkin' down that brick road this mornin',
Saw you walkin' down by that brick road this mornin',
Catchin' pebbles by some sandy beach,
Out-a reach.
Saw you early this mornin',
With your brand new boy and your Cadillac,
Saw you early this mornin',
With your brand new boy and your Cadillac,
You're goin' for something,
And I know you won't be back.
I know you're dyin' baby,
And I know you know it too,
I know you're dyin',
And I know you know it too,
Everytime I see you, I just don't know what to do.

" 'Slim Slow Slider' is about a person who is caught up in a big city like London or maybe is on dope, I'm not sure. A lot of these songs are not really personal and that's why I have to try to interpret them. A lot of them are just speculation on a subject. I think that's what most of the songs on *Astral Weeks* really are, speculation on a given theme.

Few who listened to *Astral Weeks* could escape its bittersweet romanticism, its stunningly-effective use of fresh imagery mingled with the time-honoured clichés of love, the soaring joy, the searing melancholy. It was by no means coincidental that such emotions are also the stock in trade of blues, rhythm 'n' blues, soul music, the styles constituting contemporary negro music from which Van Morrison had received so much early inspiration. Yet in this album, Morrison was able to transcend mere inspiration: these influences were manifested in his unique personal interpretation of the blues.

Astral Weeks avoided the dominant twelve- and sixteen-bar formats of traditional blues composition, and the instrumentation was similarly unrestrained, allowing highly innovative diversity. The lyrics too presented a startlingly individualistic understanding of the romantic experience. R & B lyrics tend to emphasize earthiness and raw energy: subtlety had long since been dead and buried. In the songs of *Astral Weeks*, the lyrics were intensely and dramatically subtle, often gentle to the point of genteel. One suspects they owed more to the accomplishments of the splendid British poetic tradition than to the basic urge and desires of the Southern coloured soul.

Not that they lacked fire: their very elusiveness and ingenuity forced the listener to become emotionally integrated into the stream of sound. If ever an album could sweep your mind away from the mundane and commonplace present, it was *Astral Weeks*," Van claims, "but when I wrote the songs I probably with the fervour of the most stirring religious music. And it still does. It was as if Van Morrison had taken a genuine romantic vision and recreated it in the medium of music. Few musical composers have written quite so convincingly of love and its feeling. The feeling which overwhelms all.

"I wasn't into any romantic interludes when I recorded *Astral Weeks*," Van claims, "but when I wrote the songs I probably was. I'm definitely a romantic, but I'm also a realist. Once I was speaking with a woman writer and I was getting uptight at her and then she admitted she was a total romantic. It was then I realized why I was getting uptight at her: because I'm a romantic too. I said that I was a realist at the same time and she said there's a touch of the realist in the romantic and the romantic in the realist. And it kind of evens out."

Whatever Van's intentions, it is patently obvious that *Astral Weeks* managed to eke the romanticism from almost everyone's "One time," says Van, with a look of innocence, "a guy came

Van Morrison, circa 1965

Van Morrison, at the time of Astral Weeks. *A Warner Brothers' publicity picture, 1968*

Van Morrison, in the Tupelo Honey *era. A Warner Brothers' publicity picture, 1971*

Trevor Humphries

Van Morrison in concert at London's Rainbow Theatre in the autumn of 1973

soul. It really moved people in a way they'd never known before. up to me and said that *Astral Weeks* had kept his family together." The same man subsequently named his son Domino, after the Top 40 hit from the *Street Choir* album. There are many similar stirring tales of the powerful effects of this collection of music.

What seemed to crystallize this potency was the frequent repetition of key phrases and sounds, which again has its roots in the blues vocal style. Ad-lib phrasing and scat singing are traditional emotional tools of the blues and soul genres. Listen to almost any record by Ray Charles, Aretha Franklin, B. B. King, Bobby Bland and scores of other blues vocal stylists and you can't help but note the effective use of repetition.

A track such as "Madame George" (which Van himself humbly feels is not only his greatest musical achievement thus far, but stands as one of the finest efforts of the entire pop music idiom) is a real education in how repetition can be adapted with classic grace and form. The song is not far short of overwhelming. Key mood words such as eye, goodbye, why, love, are repeated over and over, inside a softly swelling and tumbling melody, until they assume instrument tone and proportion. It's hard to think of any other vocalist black or white who has been able to achieve such a glorious union of lyric and melody, voice and instrument sound. It is as pure as it is persuasive. It lingers ever so delicately, making a keyboard of your emotions, deftly touching each chord as a spider skims across its web. It contacts lightly but the response plays havoc with one's nervous system. It is soothing and scintillating all at once. Like standing, face to the wind, in a blowing snowstorm. Opposing sensitivities in stereo: hot and cold, hard and soft, brutal and gentle, love and hate. That is how "Madame George" moves me, but I suppose I'll have to confess to being pre-conditioned. To my ear, it is the ultimate achievement of twenty years of pop music. It may well be the least harmful tranquillizer and emotion-exerciser known to technological man. It should be consumed in vast quantities by the entire population. It gives inspira to the passions and heart to nostalgia. And in my mind, it gives credence to the theory that music is the ultimate art form in terms of aesthetic response.

So, one presumes, it was no surprise that a legion of perceptive rock critics were extraordinarily moved on first exposure to *Astral Weeks*, even if the public's reaction was somewhat less vocal across record store counters. *Rolling Stone* named it the album of 1969, while in Europe Morrison was voted third most popular male artist after Otis Redding and Bob Dylan, a placing well above the Beatles, the Stones and other assorted luminaries of rock show biz. There was no shortage of ecstatic reviews from around the globe. They simply poured in, with their creators fighting among themselves to come up with the most extravagant phrases of passionate praise.

Yet for all of its brilliance (and the just recognition of such quality by the more sensitive members of the record-purchasing public), *Astral Weeks* was by no means a best-selling album. Those who did have the LP in their collections were in the minority, no matter how deeply they revered its properties. The fierce belief of the few could not overcome the bland indifference of the many. The profusion of critical support was sadly unable to turn the tide.

The trouble, I suspect, was that *Astral Weeks* was a new kind of record and it did not drop neatly into a defined category as determined by some sections of the music media and the merchandisers en masse. This album wasn't merely a scabby collection of catchy little ditties built around one accepted Top 40 riff: it was an entire concept of a vision from beginning to end. AM radio stations do not play hits of forty-minute length. It is beyond their amputated comprehension. The bastards have no soul. But they do have the broadcasting licences.

Therefore the only song from *Astral Weeks* to find its way onto the Top 40, hit-making airwaves was a version of "Slim Slow Slider" by an artist who had built a career out of cutting frequently mediocre covers of other people's songs, one Johnny Rivers. Van did not despair at his own lack of AM exposure. "I dig the way Johnny Rivers does the song because he does it like himself and he doesn't try to do it like anybody else."

FM underground, un-hit radio was still in its infancy and its influence upon album sales was nowhere near as pervasive as it is now. The FM stations certainly got right behind *Astral Weeks* but not enough record buyers were tuned in. Which eventually meant that although *Astral Weeks* is, without any doubt, among the music's finest artistic achievements, its total sales are not of sufficient quantity to even place it within the top thousand album-sellers of the past ten years. I find that in itself a tragedy of souring proportions. To realize that some of the rubbish churned out by far too many supposedly-sincere artists had eclipsed the sales and popularity of a work of genuine genius such as *Astral Weeks* is really distasteful. Executives in the music industry should hang their heads in shame. The situation reflects one of the very real flaws in the make-up of the music merchandising industry – the lack of ability to recognize real talent unless it happens to fall within previously acceptable boundaries.

Morrison simply shrugs it off as one might silently respond to a typical bad news bulletin. "Let me tell you something," he says. "I don't think a lot of people know this but when *Astral Weeks* came out, I was starving, literally. That's where that was at. I didn't really get recognition for that album until later. The critical acclaim was really good. A lot of people I knew really liked the album and I knew they weren't just putting me on. And anyway, inside I knew that it was good.

"There's a lot in between 'Gloria', 'Brown Eyed Girl' and 'Astral Weeks'. There's a lot of different things that I do and you can't get them all on one album. There's really nothing to talk about when you discuss it, because it's just the difference between art and show business."

6 On being part of the universe and into the misty: *Moondance* 1969

"*I was lost and double-crossed,*
With my hands behind my back,
I was long time hurt and thrown in the dirt,
And shoved out on the railroad track.
I was used, abused and so confused,
And I had no place to run,
But I stood and looked and my eyes got hooked,
On that beautiful morning sun,
And it seems like, and it feels like,
A Brand New Day."

There you have it in the proverbial nutshell, the story of Van Morrison's career in the music industry thus far. One doubts if a verse of any song so starkly captures the dilemma of the sensitive recording artist confronted by the mechanics of the music industry. The seemingly never-ending sludge of money crazy managers, the dishonest promoters, the absurd demands of Top 40 radio programmers, the merchandising tactics of record companies, the dismal amateurism of many segments of the media, but worst of all, the relegation of the creative force into a product not that far removed from baked beans, sliced bread or toothpaste.

It has been said many times that rock music and the industry which markets it to the public seems to attract the scum of the earth. And while you can't tar everybody with the same brush (there are *some* decent people to be found amid the rubble). Van Morrison had been running up against some notably nasty customers, with predictable results. These confrontations tend to weigh bitterly upon the creative spirit. Morrison found himself left with one of three alternatives: to quit the music industry, to grin and bear it and maybe even join it, or to make a stand and fight for his integrity. He chose the last course. He knew what he wanted to do and it was simply a case of hoping he'd get a chance of taking his shot. And since you're never beaten until you make the decision to pull out, Van figured he might as well stay in the race.

Accordingly the message of his second Warner Brothers album, *Moondance*, would appear to have been one of hope. No matter how rough the course, there are certain other factors which ultimately make the experience worthwhile: natural phenomena, the sun, the moon, the wind, the rain, the romance, nostalgia for the innocence of childhood, the entire spectrum of emotional stimuli, simply living. If restoring an air of optimism (for both himself and his audience) was one of Morrison's aims in producing *Moondance*, then he succeeded admirably. Of that there can be little doubt.

When he first began working on the material for *Moondance*, Van had no positive concept in mind, with the result that the songs extended themselves into a broad array of musical styles. Once again, and not intentionally, it was going to be virtually impossible for the industry to try and confine his talents into one tidy and trite label. *Moondance* was to be as far removed from *Astral Weeks* as a rose from a tulip. Each would have its own inimitable beauty. And furthermore, on *Moondance*, there would be no format continuity link from song to song; each would have unique style and appearance.

This profusion of musical forms confounded many observers who finally concluded that Morrison had set out to make an album which crossed as many of the predesignated boundaries as possible. He was playing with our heads, they assumed, perhaps even demonstrating with firm intent what a fallacy such barriers really are in the face of the purity of the creative force. This devilish little rebel of an Irishman had sat down and conspired to erase several musical myths. The basis of the assumption was that no single composer or artist could clothe his talents in so many different costumes. But they weren't reckoning on the depth of this particular man's ability. To him, music is music is music. And there is no room for adjectives other than in the strict qualitative sense: in short, it's either good or bad.

Morrison steadfastly insists that his only intention with *Moondance* was to produce an album of good songs. If the music happened to cover a much wider-than-usual amount of styles, this was simply the natural development in Van's personal style. He wasn't trying to prove anything by scaling a few barriers; in point of fact, he is not a subscriber to the theory that such boundaries actually exist. Rather the opposite. And with *Moondance* he provided an abundance of proof of his own conviction that all of these format barriers were devised by media and industry people who were not musicians and indeed, had precious little understanding of what music is all about.

Van started writing the songs for *Moondance* in the autumn of 1969, some ten months after the release of *Astral Weeks*. When he entered the recording studio, the only preconceived instrument arrangements were in his head. *Moondance* may sound as if every part was rehearsed a hundred times and meticulously re-arranged over and over again to achieve maximum effect. I'll agree that it's not hard to get that impression. But it's not the truth and once again, appearances can be very deceiving.

Van claims that almost everything you hear on *Moondance*, with the obvious exception of the basic song structures, was worked out inside the studio with a notably keen spirit of innovation. Head arrangements were improvised by three individuals; keyboard player Jeff Labes and the horn players Jack Schroer and Collin Tilton, along with Morrison. No set music charts were in evidence at the sessions and all of the tasteful frills to be found on *Moondance* were spontaneous ideas conceived in the A & R Studios in New York.

Even despite the fact that most of the *Moondance* vocals were recorded live, the overall production was not sufficiently live for Van's personal taste. With hindsight he said in 1973 that he would have preferred to have cut the entire album in a live setting. "I'd like to have done it live. I'd like to have got the same musicians again and recorded the album live. That would have been a killer. But the musicians weren't the sort of guys who work live gigs, they only work in the studio. I guess the reason that *Moondance* is more of a band album, Van Morrison with the band sort of thing, is because that was the type of band that I dig. Two horns and a rhythm section: they're the type of bands that I like best."

None of the musicians who played on *Astral Weeks*, with the exception of Morrison himself, were involved in the *Moondance* sessions. The complete line-up included Jack Schroer (alto and soprano sax), Collin Tilton (tenor sax and flute), Jeff Labes (keyboards), John Platania (guitar), John Klingberg (bass), Gary Malabar (drums), Guy Masson (congas) and a girl back-up vocal group which consisted of Emily Houston (of the Sweet Inspirations), Judy Clay (who had several hit singles for Atlantic with Billy Vera), and Jackie Verdell.

Schroer, Labes and Platania were to have lengthy relationships with Van, while Klingberg would play on just one further album. "I met Jack Schroer in New York when I heard him play in a blues band and I invited him to play on a gig with me the next night. He did and he's been with me ever since." The blues band which both Schroer and Collin Tilton had played in was the Colwell-Winfield Blues Band – they can be heard on a Verve/Forecast album entitled *Cold Wind Blows*, released in 1968. Schroer had also completed some sessions with Boz Scaggs, an artist whose publicists are fond of claiming that Scaggs is in the Van Morrison mould. Guitarist John Platania first met Van in Woodstock early in 1969, and by coincidence, he had also been signed to Bang Records as a member of the Silver Bicycle.

Moondance was released by Warner Brothers in February 1970, a few weeks before Paul McCartney announced the demise of the Beatles. To explore the individual songs, it seems necessary to look again to Morrison's own comments.

AND IT STONED ME

Half a mile from the county fair and rain came pourin' down,
Me and Billy standing there with a silver half a crown,
Hands are full of a fishin' rod and the tackle on our backs,
We just stood there gettin' wet with our backs against the fence.
Oh the water, oh the water, oh the water,
Hope it don't rain all day.
And It Stoned Me to my soul,
Stoned me just like a jelly roll, And It Stoned Me.
And It Stoned Me to my soul,
Stoned me just like goin' home, And It Stoned Me.

Then the rain let up and the sun came up and we were gettin' dry,
Almost glad a pickup truck nearly passed us by.
So we jumped right in and the driver grinned and he dropped us on the road,
We looked at the swim and we jumped right in not to mention fishing poles.
Oh the water, oh the water, oh the water,
Let it run all over me.

On the way back home we sang a song but our throats were gettin' dry,
Then we saw the man from across the road with the sunshine in his eye.
Well he lived all alone in his little home with a great big gallon jar,
There were bottle two one for me and you and he said 'Hey there you are.'
Oh the water, oh the water, oh the water,
Get it myself from the mountain stream.

" 'And It Stoned Me'," says Van, "is about a real experience. It's just about being stoned off nature. You know, remembering how it was when you were a kid and just got stoned from nature and you didn't need anything else."

MOONDANCE

Well it's a marvellous night for a Moondance,
With the stars up above in your eyes,
A fantabulous night to make romance,
'Neath the cover of October skies.
And all the leaves on the trees are falling,
To the sound of the breezes that blow,
And I'm trying to please to the calling,
Of your heart-strings that play soft and low.

And all the night's magic seems to whisper and hush,
And all the soft moonlight seems to shine in your blush.
Can I just have one more Moondance with you, my love?
Can I just make some more romance with you, my love?

Well I wanna make love to you tonight,
I can't wait till the morning has come,
And I know now the time is just right,
And straight into my arms you will run.
And when you come my heart will be waiting,
To make sure that you're never alone,
There and then all my dreams will come true dear,
There and then I will make you my own.
And everytime I touch you, you just tremble inside,
And I know how much you want me that you can't hide.
Can I just have one more Moondance with you, my love?
Can I just make some more romance with you, my love?

One more Moondance with you in the moonlight,
On a magic night,
La-la-la-la in the moonlight,
On a magic night,
Can't I just have one more dance with you my love?

"With 'Moondance', I wrote the melody first. I played the melody on a soprano sax and I knew I had a song so I wrote lyrics to go with the melody. That's the way I wrote that one. I don't really have any words to particularly describe the song, sophisticated is probably the word I'm looking for. For me, 'Moondance' is a sophisticated song. Frank Sinatra wouldn't be out of place singing that."

CRAZY LOVE

I can hear her heartbeat for a thousand miles,
And the heavens open every time she smiles,
And when I come to her that's where I belong,
Yes I'm running to her like a river's song.

She gives me love, love, love, love, Crazy Love,
She gives me love, love, love, love, Crazy Love,

She's got a fine sense of humor when I'm feelin' lowdown,
And when I come to her when the sun goes down,
She takes away my trouble, takes away my grief,
Takes away my heartache in the night like a thief.

And I need her in the day time,
And I need her in the night,
And I want to throw my arms around her,
And kiss her, hug her, kiss her, hug her tight.
And when I'm returning from so far away,
She gives me such sweet lovin' brightens up my day,
And it makes me righteous, and it makes me whole,
And it makes me mellow down to my soul.

" 'Crazy Love' is about basically what it says it's about."

CARAVAN

And the Caravan is on its way,
I can hear the merry gypsies play,
Mama look at Amarou,
She's a-playing with the radio.

And the Caravan has all my friends,
It will stay with me until the end,
Gypsy Robin, sweet Amarou,
Tell me everything I want to know.

Turn up your radio and let 'em hear your song,
Switch on your electric light and we can get down to what
is really wrong,
I long to hold you tight so I can feel you,
Sweet lady of the night your eyes shall reveal you.

If you will turn it up, turn it up,
Little bit higher, radio,
Turn it up, turn it up,
So you know, radio,
So you know, s'got so radio,
Radio turn it up.

And the Caravan is painted red and white,
That means everybody's staying overnight,
Now the barefoot gypsy boys 'round the campfire sing
 and play,
And a woman tells us of her ways.

" 'Caravan' is getting back into the romanticism bit with gypsies and all that. I'm really fascinated by gypsies . . . I love them. The part about the radio came when I was actually writing the song. I was living in the country (near Woodstock) and the nearest house was way, way down the road. Yet somehow I could hear a radio coming from somewhere. We were here and they were way down there, yet I could hear their radio like it was in the same room. I don't know how to explain it. There was some story about an underground passage under the house I was living in . . . rumours from kids and stuff and I was beginning to think it was true. How can you hear someone's radio from a mile away, as if it was playing in your own house? So I *had* to put that into the song. It was a must."

INTO THE MYSTIC

We were born before the wind,
Also younger than the sun,
Ere the bonny boat was one,
As we sailed Into The Mystic.

Hark now hear the sailor's cry,
Smell the sea and feel the sky,
Let your soul and spirit fly,
Into The Mystic.

And when the foghorn blows,
I will be coming home,
And when the foghorn blows,
I want to hear it, I don't have to fear it.
And I want to rock your gypsy soul,
Just like way back in the days of old,
And together we will fold,
Into The Mystic.

" 'Into The Mystic'," observes Van, "is another one like 'Madame Joy' and 'Brown Skinned Girl'. Originally I wrote it as Into The Misty. But later I thought that it had something of an ethereal feeling to it so I called it 'Into The Mystic'. That song is kind of funny because when it came time to send the lyrics into Warner Brothers Music, I couldn't figure our just what to send them. Because really the song has two sets of lyrics. For example there's 'I was born before the wind' and 'I was borne before the wind' . . . and 'Also younger than the son, Ere the bonny boat was one' and 'All so younger than the son, Ere the bonny boat was won.' It had all these different meanings and they were all in there: whatever one you want is in the song. I guess the song is just about being part of the universe."

COME RUNNING

By the side of this track when this train goes by,
The wind and rain will catch you,
You will sigh deep in your heart,
Then you'll Come Running to me, you'll Come Running
to me.

Well you watch the train goin' round the bend,
Play in dust and dream that it will never end,
Deep in your heart,
Then you Come a-Running to me, you'll Come Running to
me.

I said hey, Come Running to me,
Oh Come a-Running to me,
Hey, baby Come a-Running to me,
I said hey, Come Running to me,
Oh Come Running to me.
Ho there, Come a-running to me,

With your hound dog by your side,
And your arms just open wide,
I wanna keep you satisfied,
In the morning sun by my side,
Come on, come on run, all right.

Well you kick the sand up with your heels,
You think to yourself how good it feels,
Farewell your walkin' shoes,
Then you'll Come Running to me, you'll Come Running to Me.

"Starting on side two, 'Come Running' is a very light type of song. It's not too heavy. It's just a happy-go-lucky song. There are no messages or anything like that."

THESE DREAMS OF YOU

I dreamt you paid your dues in Canada,
And left me to come through.
I head for the right way,
I knew exactly just what to do.
I dreamed we played cards in the dark,
And you lost and you lied;
Wasn't very hard to do,
But hurt me deep down inside.
These Dreams of You, so real and so true,
These Dreams of You, so real and so true.

My back was up against the wall,
And you slowly just walked away,
You never really heard my call,
When I cried out that way.
You pointed out for me to go;
Then you said I was the one,
Had to reap what you did sow.

And hushabye, don't ever think about it,
Go to sleep don't ever say one word,
Close your eyes you are an angel,
Sent here from above.

And Ray Charles was shot down,
But he got up to do his best.
A crowd of people gathered round,
To the question answered "Yes".
You slapped me on the face,
I turned around the other cheek,
You couldn't really stand the pace,
And I would never be so meek.

" 'These Dreams of You' was the result of a dream I had about Ray Charles being shot down. That started off the whole song. The line 'you paid your dues in Canada' . . . I don't really know where that comes from. I just have a romantic image of going to Canada and that's about it. The song is basically about dreams."

BRAND NEW DAY

When all the dark clouds roll away,
And the sun begins to shine,
I see my freedom from across the way,
And it comes right in on time.
Well it shines so bright,
And it gives so much light,

And it comes from the sky above,
Makes me feel so free,
Makes me feel like me,
And it lights my life with love.
And it seems like, and it feels like,
And it seems like,
A Brand New Day, a Brand New Day.

I was lost and I was crossed,
With my hands behind my back,
I was long time hurt and thrown in the dirt,
And shoved out on the railroad track.
I been used, abused,
And so confused,
And I had no place to run.
But I stood and looked,
And my eyes got hooked,
On that beautiful morning sun.

And the sun shines down around on all the ground,
Yeah and the grass is oh so green,
And my heart is still and I've got the will,
And I don't really feel so mean.
Here it comes, here it comes,
Here it comes right now,
And it comes right in on time.
Well it eases me,
And it pleases me,
And it satisfies my mind.

" 'Brand New Day' expressed a lot of hope. It was really weird when I wrote the song. I was in Boston and having a hard job getting myself up spiritually. I couldn't relate to anything I heard on the radio. I'd listen to FM. And get the same thing every day and every night. Then one day this song came on the FM station and it had this particular feeling and this particular groove and it was totally fresh. It seemed to me like things were making sense. You know what I mean, things were starting to make sense as far as the music was concerned. The drums were playing really laid back and I didn't know who the hell the artist was. It turned out that it was The Band.

"I'd been sitting on the grass across the street from where I lived before the record came on. I was just sitting over there and I looked up at the sky and the sun started to shine and all of a sudden, the song just came through my head. So I went into the house and I started to write it down, right from 'When all the dark clouds roll away.' I'd turned on the radio and I'd heard that song and I just thought that something was happening. The song was either 'The Weight' or 'I Shall Be Released'; I think it was the latter."

EVERYONE

We shall walk again down along the lane,
Down the avenue just like we used to do.
With out heads so high smile at passers by,
Then we'll softly sigh:
Everyone, Everyone, Everyone,
Everyone, Everyone, Everyone, Everyone.

By the winding stream, we shall lie and dream,
We'll make dreams come true if we want them to.
And so overcome play the pipes and drum,
Sing a happy song and we'll sing along.

" 'Everyone' is just a song of hope, that's what that is."

GLAD TIDINGS

And they'll lay you down low and easy,
And the lips that you kiss will say Christmas,
And the miles that you've travelled the distance,
So believe no lies, dry your eyes,
And realize, that surprise.

And the business will shake hands and talk in numbers,
And the princess will wake up from her slumbers,
And all the knights will step forth with their armbands,
And every stranger you meet in the street will make
demands.

And we'll send you Glad Tidings from New York,
Open up your eyes so you may see,
Ask you not to read between the lines,
Hope that you will come right in on time.

And they'll talk to you while you're in trances,
And you'll visualize not taking any chances,
But meet them halfway with love peace and persuasion,
And expect them to rise for the occasion.
And it gratifies when you see it materialize,
In front of your eyes, by surprise.

And they'll lay you down low and easy.

" 'Glad Tidings' is just about a period of time in which I was living in New York. A friend of mine wrote me a letter from London and he'd written on the envelope: 'Glad Tidings from London.' So I wrote Glad Tidings from New York and that's where I got the idea."

Moondance was the first album on which Van Morrison was officially listed as producer. Lewis Merenstein, the producer of *Astral Weeks*, was relegated to the position of executive producer. Van subsequently explained that the reason he chose to produce *Moondance* himself was because he couldn't find anyone else to do it. He was living in Woodstock at the time and several potential producers came up to discuss the project, but Van was less than impressed. "No one knew what I was looking for except me, so I just did it." In the mixing phase of the operation, he acknowledged considerable assistance from two staff engineers at the A & R Studios, Elliot Scheiner and Tony May.

Moondance reached the number 29 position on the Billboard best-selling charts and produced a minor single hit, "Come Running". Warner Brothers report that it has now sold "well over 300,000 copies", easily twice as many as *Astral Weeks* but still about 100,000 copies short of American gold album status. *Moondance* also garnered many exceptional reviews.

Writing in the *San Francisco Chronicle*, the astute jazz/rock critic Ralph J. Gleason noted: "It is really in the quality of his sound that Van Morrison's impact comes through most strongly. He wails. He wails as the jazz musicians speak of wailing, as the gypsies, as the Gaels and the old folks in every culture speak of it. He gets a quality of intensity in that wail which really hooks your mind, carries you along with his voice as it rises and falls in long, soaring lines."

Fusion magazine reviewer Gary von Tersch claimed: "Van Morrison's music runs in the veins of this new decade and his brand of persuasion and optimism is what we urgently need in these times of Chicago, Sinclair and Seale."

Greil Marcus and Lester Bangs of *Rolling Stone* concluded: "*Moondance* is an album of musical invention and lyrical confidence; the strong moods of 'Into The Mystic' and the fine, epic brilliance of 'Caravan' will carry it past many good records we'll forget in the next few years."

Zig Zag magazine's John Tobler, in an overview evaluation, added: "I cannot tell you too strongly just how extra-terrestrially brilliant it all is." And *The Times*' resident Morrison freak, Myles Palmer, properly observed in his 1973 piece: "*Astral Weeks* and *Moondance* – both equally distinguished works – were as different as consecutive albums by the same singer could possibly be. They contain some of the most original, stylish and durable music of our time, and placed him immediately in the first rank of rock artists."

In one sense, *Astral Weeks* and *Moondance* had combined to raise Morrison's following, small perhaps by superstar standards, to a near fanatical level. And I suspect that what this cult may have lacked in numerical strength was more than compensated for by the depth of emotion his listeners felt about Morrison's music. *Moondance* was to some ears a more accessible album than its predecessor, but others find no common ground on which to compare the two.

The diversity of styles contained in *Moondance* helped to break down many barriers which had restricted his music in the *Astral Weeks* era. With his second Warner Brothers album, he gained valuable radio exposure in jazz and middle-of-the-road formats, enlarging his audience at the top end of the age scale. "But it's not really a new thing at all," Van insisted in 1971, as regards the *Moondance* diversity. "It's just that I do a lot of different styles. You can't really put all different styles on one album. So with each new album I try to show another style. An album is just so much. It's just forty minutes and I can't get all my music on one album so I try to vary it as much as I can so I can do things I want. Eventually I'd like to record live: it's a true form."

In November 1973, I asked Van which of the *Moondance* tracks now worked best to his ear and he had absolutely no hesitation in naming "Brand New Day". "It's the one that says it for me because it's still saying it right now. In fact it's saying it more now than it did when I recorded it. When I cut it, it wasn't saying it the way it is now. For some reason it's really saying it to me now. I really feel in touch with that song . . . more than I've ever felt about it."

7 Where someone was on his back to get something cranked out: *His Band and The Street Choir* 1970

Most members of the Van Morrison cult agree that the man is supremely talented. Unlike so many of the superstars of mid-seventies' rock, Morrison made it purely and simply on the strength of this talent. He's never received much boost from an industry which he openly despises for its crass commercialism and unbridled greed.

A lesser talent would have long since been gobbled up and ground underfoot by an angry industry, or by his own disillusionment. Yet Morrison continued to compose sweeter melodies than almost any songwriter in rock; his lyrics were as sensitive and as compelling as anything written in his time; his skill at musical arranging was all but incomparable (and he really did seem to bring out the best in normally disinterested session musicians); and his vocal efforts were in a class of their own. He appeared to many to be the ultimate hybrid of the singing-songwriter genre.

The larger his talent grew before the eyes of those who were becoming increasingly familiar with his recorded music, the more people wanted to know about Van Morrison the person. This curiosity seemed insatiable and it was fuelled by a chronic shortage of media information about Morrison. You simply didn't read many interviews with him or even feature articles about him. His profile, elusive and evasive, was as laid back as any artist in rock. Consequently many myths began to form around his image, or lack of one. The less he said to the press the more they wanted to invent their own images. Assumptions unlimited were the order of the day. It appeared that people (some members of the press included) were so profoundly moved by their own emotional reactions to Morrison's music that they felt compelled to create an extraordinary rationale to appease their minds.

As I was saying earlier, Morrison is a very special individual in many ways and this is by no means confined to his music. In fact I would dare to admit that what I personally most admire about the man is his ruthless dedication to honesty and integrity. These may be fairly outmoded virtues in the context of the music industry per se but I'll risk being labelled as hopelessly unhip by confessing that their presence among Morrison's character traits impresses me. His outlook manifests itself in several ways which I shall endeavour to unveil as we progress.

At this juncture however I should like to draw your attention to his fierce disregard for blundering arses of media interviewers, of which he appears to have experienced a greater number than most of his colleagues (a judgment made on the relative number of complaints by other artists). Now I'll readily claim that I too have asked my fair share of stupid and banal questions over the years. Nobody's perfect and least of all us over-bloated practitioners of the profession of rock commentary. It's really a question of the appropriate time and place: an interviewer can be forgiven the occasional dumb remark while stretched out on the floor of some Holiday Inn hotel in the downtown of God knows where with a group of rock 'n' roll musicians and you're all as high as kites. You do your devoted best but it does happen at times that the current circumstances can be quite overpowering. Immunity is hard to maintain without being obnoxious. And so frozen noses, waves of nausea, fried brains, creepie-crawlies in your pink-striped underpants: these then are a sample of the occupational hazards of the dutiful rock scribe.

Yet despite the difficulties, there can be no justification for shoddy professionalism: lack of reasonable research, ignorance of relevant basic facts, waffle, tasteless questioning, undue assumptions, pseudo-hipness and so on. The rock writing scene, I'm afraid, is well known to be plagued by such things. Some journalists seem to thrive on them. Van Morrison, as you might have guessed by now, is one artist who will not tolerate these standards and I should like to commend him for it.

Over the years Morrison has acquired a wholly-undeserved reputation as a "difficult interview", an "impossible subject", a "hopeless prick", an "explosive personality", an "unpredictable bad-tempered bastard" (various descriptions which have been expressed within my hearing); all of which I find to be horseshit. One attempts not to be influenced by the opinion of others in making character judgments and I can only state that my own interview sessions with Van Morrison have been notably free of the above difficulties. Which I suppose does lead one to presume that some of one's colleagues might not be approaching the subject in a suitable manner.

For one thing, Morrison usually reacts strongly to stupid questions. He has never been afraid of incurring the wrath of a member of the press. If you ask an ignorant question, you're more than likely to receive a forceful answer. As well you should. Unwarranted assumptions annoy him more than anything else. He is seldom patient or polite in replying to questions of this nature.

It seems pointless to identify any particular interviews but in the course of conducting the research for this book, I have come across some of the most uninformed and unskilled questioning imaginable and I am amazed that Morrison didn't haul off and bop a few beaks. Not all such media people are necessarily ill-intentioned; indeed many people approach a Morrison interview with such an obvious spirit of reverence that I strongly suspect it bewilders the subject. The point remains that being sympathetic to Morrison's music is not sufficient excuse for stupidity. The man just won't tolerate it and I feel he has ample justification.

There is no way an interviewer can waffle through a rap with Van Morrison. It either clicks or it falls flat: there are no half-measures. As a result, many media people will continue to portray the man as some sort of chronically-agitated St. George, mounted on his pure white steed, itching for the arrival of any poor interviewer with malice pumping in his breast and his soul burning with an insatiable desire to revenge past blood. Thus the myths survive.

As it turns out in reality, Morrison can be one of the most rewarding interviewees in the rock scene. He knows his music and he's fully aware of the directions in which it's going. More significantly, he does not beat around the bush by weaving a blanket of pat answers. He really says what he thinks and if this tends to shock some interviewers, then let that be a vital lesson in the pitfalls of preconceived notions and idiotic assumptions.

Above all Morrison can be relied upon to provide an astoundingly-objective view of his own career, to the point of making statements which the more orthodox members of the music industry would consider detrimental to their own pockets. I've even heard it said that Morrison makes media comments which are self-destructive—true, they are seldom couched in uncertain terms. But I'm still naïve enough to believe that adherence to honesty does little damage in the long run.

In the case of his third album for Warner Brothers, *Van Morrison: His Band and The Street Choir*, Van is brutally honest. By the time the album recording was begun (the early summer of 1970) Van was hung up amidst management changes and reorganization of his affairs in general, and he found himself confronted once again by the pressures of the record industry.

Of course all of these hassles were proceeding well behind the scenes. Out front everybody seemed to be talking now about this whiz kid from Ireland, this Belfast Cowboy as Robbie Robertson had nicknamed him, a face from the British R & B boom past who had produced not one but two stunningly beautiful albums. Even people who had not heard more than a track or two from *Astral Weeks* and *Moondance* somehow *knew* they were fantastic because everybody appeared to be of that opinion.

A certain lingering mystique had built up around his name (except in England where the media and fellow musicians claimed to be confused through their memories of Van's Them association) and the long-awaited release of his *Street Choir* album was greeted by a howl of instantaneous media acclaim.

Now not for a second would I wish to imply that every writer who waxed favourably about the *Street Choir* LP had neglected to listen to either *Astral Weeks* or *Moondance*; but I do find it imperative to attempt to capture the Morrison momentum evident in this period. He'd produced two remarkable albums in a row which had affectionately endeared him to more perceptive quarters of the media. He was, when you get right down to it, the epitome of early seventies' radical chic, absolutely in with the in crowd, riding high with the war children jet set, sailing across the dirt tracks of southern Asia in painted letters on the dusty side panels of Kombie vans . . . those epic voyages in *Astral Weeks*, keeping families together, metronoming so many passionate strokes on the darkened couch, inspiring unions of joy in a devastated age, igniting rare passions in jaded flesh. *Shit he had it made.* To the people who are obsessed with maintaining a breathless pace in front of "the mob", Van Morrison was the course celebrity, the raison d'être. Dropping his name was like a password to the next world, you were *there*, right on brother, doing you own thing, far fucking out, taking the first toke, giving out the good word, blowing everyone's mind (or what remained of them). You had balls and bangles all at once if you were into Van Morrison in the opening months of the seventies. Dylan, Arlo Guthrie, Donovan, Janis, Stephen Stills, Richie Havens . . . *everybody* knew about them, you only had to switch on your radio and they blurted out anthems of amiability, it was all so low class. But Van Morrison, that cat from Ireland where there was all that crazy murder going down, the first real rocker from generations of monstrously mad poets, now *he* was the zenith of fashionable. You just couldn't put a clogged-foot wrong with Van Morrison. He was hip and groovy. And, most of all, *ahead*.

The rock press knew it. Never let it be said that many critics let objectivity obstruct their vision of Van Morrison circa spring 1970. Subjectivity was the tune of the season. The reviews glittered with superlatives. Van the man had done it again, man.

Observed *Rolling Stone*'s Jon Landau, *Street Choir* is a "free album. It was recorded with minimal overdubbing and was obviously intended to show the other side of Morrison." To Landau's ear, it was "another beautiful phase in the continuing development of one of the few originals left in rock . . . the song he is singing keeps getting better and better."

ZigZag magazine's John Tobler was not quite so overwhelmed. He ventured the opinion that "even if it's inferior to *Moondance*, it's still better than eighty per cent of the records you've got in your collection."

Even the drones of Top 40 radio were impressed. After all but ignoring both *Astral Weeks* and *Moondance*, "Domino" turned out to be Van's biggest singles hit since "Brown Eyed Girl", and "Blue Money" also sold a few hundred thousand copies. The AM exposure of Morrison undoubtedly was a major contributor in the *Street Choir* album exceeding the 200,000 sales mark (and still standing as his third top-selling LP to date).

Street Choir also marked the recording debut of an entity known as the Caledonia Soul Orchestra, which would exist for at least the next six albums in name if not personnel. Perhaps more significantly, it represented the arrival of drummer Dahaud Elias Shaar (sometimes referred to as David Shaw) who subsequently emerged through Morrison's encouragement and his own skills as one of the most innovative drummers in contemporary music. Other musicians forming the Caledonia Soul Orchestra at this time include *Moondance* veterans Jack Schroer on alto and soprano sax, guitarist John Platania and

John Klingberg on bass, along with Keith Johnson (trumpet and organ, a refugee of sorts from the Butterfield Blues Band), Alan Hand (keyboards, and of course what else!), and the aforementioned Dahaud Shaar, who doubled up on bass clarinet and in backing vocals on the "Blue Money" track.

The Street Choir comprised Janet Planet, Mrs. Ellen Schroer, Martha Velez, Andy Robinson and Larry Goldsmith. In addition, the girl trio from the *Moondance* sessions, Emily Houston, Judy Clay and Jackie Verdell, performed on "If I Ever Needed Someone".

Yet, to my ear anyway, the *Street Choir* album in essence lacked the conviction of *Astral Weeks* and *Moondance*. It did not aspire to the frothy brilliance of either. It seemed to be without purpose or power when compared with the two earlier albums. Nor did it possess their durability.

Therefore I was not totally surprised when Morrison had some quite searing comments to offer on the subject of the *Street Choir* album late in 1973. "I really don't think that album is saying much," he said rather emphatically. "There really isn't anything I'm saying there. Later on I realized what the song 'Street Choir' meant. When I wrote it I didn't have a clue. Later on when I looked at it, I picked up on it. That album is like a kick in the head or something.

"It was originally a concept to do an acapella album . . . 'Street Choir' was to be an acapella group. I wanted these certain guys to form an acapella group so that I could cut a lot of songs acapella with just maybe one guitar. But it didn't turn out; it all got weird.

"First of all, there was the title of the album. Somewhere along the line I lost control of that album. Somebody else got control of it and got the cover and all that shit while I was out on the West Coast. I knew what was happening to it, but it was like I couldn't stop it. I'd given my business thing over to someone else and although I had final approval on things, they just went ahead and did the wrong thing. They told the record company it was one way and it wasn't. So that whole thing went wrong.

"I'd rather not think about that album because it doesn't mean much in terms of where I was at. It was the sort of thing where someone was on my back to get something cranked out, even though they knew it was wrong. A couple of songs on it were hit singles but the album didn't sell very well and I'm glad."

8 An initial concept for a Country & Western album but ultimately a bunch of songs that were left over from before: *Tupelo Honey* 1971

A reasonable indication of Van Morrison's talent can be gained from the fact that even his second-rate material, by his own definition, is still eminently capable of whipping up a thick froth of press fervour. While many top-selling artists appear to have difficulty in receiving even a modicum of good press with their finest work, Morrison is in the enviable position of drawing a storm of acclaim with virtually anything he records. Critics appear to drop the reins of objectivity when a new Van Morrison album arrives at their doorstep, they approach their task with what would appear to be highly favourable preconceptions. It probably has something to do with the deep impact made by *Astral Weeks* and *Moondance*: any artist capable of achieving those standards could not conceivably make a bad record again. One can think of dozens of successful acts who would likely donate half their fortunes to charity to be assured of a similar media regard.

We have already seen how *Street Choir*, an album for which Morrison himself has little love, was accorded considerable press acclaim. *Tupelo Honey*, his fourth album for Warner Brothers, could be said to fall into much the same category. It too is a production which Van all but disclaims, yet the press reaction was quite spectacular. Obviously the man could do no wrong.

At the end of winter 1971 Van's house lease in Woodstock expired and since the owner wanted to move in some friends, Morrison decided to head for California with his family. Setting himself up in Marin County just north of San Francisco, Van had vague ideas of recording a country and western-oriented album. Several tracks had already been put down in Woodstock but Van wasn't too delighted with the results.

The musicians assembled for those sessions and several which followed in San Francisco had included the return of former Modern Jazz Quartet drummer, Connie Kay (he was one of the many highlights of *Astral Weeks*), sax player Jack Schroer and drummer Gary Malabar (of *Moondance* fame). The new faces comprised guitarist Ronnie Montrose (who has since gained prominence with Edgar Winter's White Trash and his own Montrose band), Bill Church on bass, drummer Rick Schlosser (who played with Link Wray), keyboards player Mark Jordon (since with Dave Mason), Lui s Gasca on trumpet, "Boots" Stuart Houston and Bruce Royston on flutes, John McFee (of the San Francisco group, Clover) on pedal steel guitar, and Ted Templeman on organ. Templeman was a former member of Harpers Bizarre, an Ivy League-ish group which clicked in the late sixties with Paul Simon's "59th Street Bridge song (Feeling Groovy)". The backing vocals were supplied by Janet Planet Ellen Schroer, Ronnie Montrose, "Boots" Stuart Houston and Van.

Ted Templeman, who had joined the staff of Warner Brothers' Artists & Repertoire department, was listed as co-producer although Morrison prefers to regard him as the technical adviser.

Tupelo Honey was released in October 1971, exactly a year after the *Street Choir* LP, and it ultimately reached the number 27 position on the *Billboard* best-selling charts, five positions higher than its predecessor. What is most astounding about *Tupelo Honey* however is the sales it achieved. By mid-1974, the album was "well over the 350,000 mark" making it the top-selling album in Morrison's career, a solid 50,000 copies ahead of *Moondance*. Van was less than impressed: to him it represented the ultimate irony in the recording scene, the sad fact that the best seldom rose to the surface.

"I wasn't very happy with *Tupelo Honey*," he said recently. "It consisted of songs that were left over from before (earlier sessions) and that they'd finally gotten around to using. It wasn't really fresh. It was a whole bunch of songs that had been hanging around for a while. I was really trying to make a country and western album.

"I never really listen to *Tupelo Honey* much . . . I just don't connect up with it. I've got a bad taste in my mouth for both the *Street Choir* and *Tupelo Honey* albums."

The critics didn't seem to pick up on it. *Rolling Stone*'s Jon Landau noted: "On the first few plays, *Tupelo Honey* might strike the casual listener as merely a superior collection of pop tunes, but every repeated play reveals its deeper level of meaning. For nine songs, Van consistently and consciously develops the theme of 'starting a new life' through the growth of his own strength and confidence. *Tupelo Honey* is in one sense but another example of the artist making increased use of the album as the unit of communication as opposed to merely the song or the cut. Everything on it is perfectly integrated."

In London, *Time Out*'s Ian Hoare, in an overview article, concluded that "*Tupelo Honey*, in particular, is a summit." *Zig Zag*'s John Tobler said: 'If all music were as good as this, there would be no need for anybody to make any more, because this is the real thing."

Several of Morrison's music contemporaries obviously agreed. Richie Havens recorded a version of the title song, Martha Reeves and the Vandellas cut "Wild Night", and "I Wanna Roo You" was recorded by Dusty Springfield, Jackie DeShannon and Goldie Hawn.

If not much else, *Tupelo Honey* was an incessantly romantic album and perhaps people were willing to overlook a comparative lack of aesthetic quality in return for a collection which seemed dedicated to the grand stroke. Of course much of Morrison's music has wandered into the domain of romance but it might be fairly stated that *Tupelo Honey* carried the theme to excessive gulps of love and devotion. The album jacket (which Van's manager at the time informed him would be "cute") brandished an image-making full colour pic of Van leading his lady love, Janet Planet, on horseback down a tree-roofed country lane. Love glistened from the leaves. It was so embracing that it would have seemed hopelessly pretentious in a lesser artist. But this was the Van Morrison lifestyle, wasn't it?

Later Morrison was at pains to dispel some of the images which people found themselves getting behind as a result of what radiated from the *Tupelo Honey* jacket; and in particular the widespread critical assumption that the LP was dedicated to Janet Planet. "The picture was taken at a stable and I didn't live there," he said. "We just went there and took the picture and split. A lot of people seem to think that album covers are your life or something." But in the absence of much information on Morrison in the media, the public followed the existing paths laid down in the merchandising of his music.

Despite Morrison's lack of regard for *Tupelo Honey*, it seemed difficult to totally dismiss the entire collection of songs. "Moonshine Whiskey", in particular, which Van later admitted he'd written for "Janis Joplin or something", shines through with much of the grace which dominated earlier work. "Old Old

Woodstock" was effective too in its capture of an already trodden-on lifestyle.

Overall the point that really arises from *Tupelo Honey* is that even when he's not at his best, Van Morrison is still superior to a large percentage of the material bulldozed out into the market by misunderstanding record companies, trying to catch up on existing trends. In his top notch, Morrison is the finest in his class. Yet when circumstances are not to his liking, he is still able to lay down what many other artists would be proud to call a personal triumph. It's all a matter of relativity.

9 Getting back into what he was trying to do: *Saint Dominic's Preview* 1972

When it's all boiled down and the hums of hindsight are ringing in your ears, Van Morrison's fifth album for Warner Brothers *Saint Dominic's Preview* is the real successor to *Moondance.* Those industry words "follow-up", "follow-on", "latest release" are hackneyed clichés, but since Van claims he does not "connect up" with either *Street Choir* or *Tupelo Honey* then it can be rightly assumed that the line started with *Astral Weeks* and *Moondance* leads next to *Saint Dominic's Preview.* The thirty months which separated *Moondance* and *Saint Dominic's Preview* are not indicative of the real proximity of these albums in Morrison's artistic flow.

Released in July 1972, *Saint Dominic's Preview* was destined to become Van's highest-charted album so far and sales are now over the 200,000 mark in the States. This new album was to sell twice as many copies as *Astral Weeks* but less than *Moondance, Street Choir* and *Tupelo Honey.* Originally to be titled *Green* (a connection with a song which would ultimately be included on the following album), this LP was named *Saint Dominic's Preview* after Van wrote the title tune. It is interesting to discover that Saint Dominic is generally acknowledged as being the institutor of the Inquisition, one of the dirtiest stains upon the flag of Christianity.

In its extremely favourable profile of Van in June 1972, *Rolling Stone* quoted Van as stating the title song had emerged from a dream he'd experienced concerning a Saint Dominic's church where people had collected to take part in a mass for peace in Northern Ireland. Later, *Stone* claimed, Van was playing a gig at the Univeristy of Nevada in Reno when he read a newspaper article about a mass to be held the following day at Saint Dominic's Church in San Francisco.

A year on in time, Morrison vehemently denied the implications. "I didn't have a dream," he insisted to *Zig Zag*'s John Tobler in London. "The writer said that I had a dream about a mass in church. I didn't have a dream. The only thing that happened was I mentioned to the writer that I'd seen in the paper that there was a service in Saint Dominic's Church in San Francisco. That was all I said and the writer did the rest. This was after I wrote the song. I just mentioned I saw the name in a paper and the writer made up the rest." These inconsistencies tend to confuse even further the spirit of mystique which surrounds Morrison and which he maintains is an enigma to him. The line which separates fact from fiction wears awfully thin around Van Morrison.

Whatever the origins of its title, *Saint Dominic's Preview* was a brilliant album by any yardstick. Lyrically it covered much new ground (even lightly touching on Van's disdain for the trendy herds which tramp around the rock scene press party circuit) and two tracks in particular, "Almost Independence Day" and "Listen to the Lion", were emotional echoes of Van's glorious peaks in "Madame George". In use of diverse instrumentation, *Saint Dominic's Preview* was probably his most adventurous, avant garde album to date, including of all things a hugely impressive Moog synthesizer. One doubted if the Moog had ever been used so judiciously and effectively as a rock instrument.

The musicians were grouped together under the name of the Caledonia Soul Orchestra and consisted of assorted Van Morrison touring musicians and session cats, which included Bill Church and Leroy Vinegar on bass; Rick Schlosser, Gary Malabar and Connie Kay on drums; Jack Schroer, Jules Broussard and "Boots" Rolf Houston on saxes; Mark Jordon, Mark Naftalin and Doug Messenger on guitars; steel guitarist John McFee; Pat O'Hara on trombone; and Bernie Krause on Moog. Back vocals were contributed by Mark Springer, Ronnie Montrose, Janet Planet, Ellen Schroer, and B. R. Houston. Mark Naftalin had previously gigged with Paul Butterfield and Mike Bloomfield, Ron Elliot had been a member of the Beau Brummels (a San Francisco group of "Laugh Laugh" fame), and Jules Broussard performed on Boz Scaggs albums.

Saint Dominic's Preview zoomed off in dynamic style with the driving rhythm number "Jackie Wilson Said (I'm in Heaven When You Smile)", although the hook line is "Let it all hang out", an affectionate tribute to an old influence. Van claimed to have been a long-time fan of Jackie Wilson (whose greatest single include "Lonely Teardrops", "Reet Petite", "Higher and Higher", "Baby Workout", "Doggin' Around" and "Danny

Boy") and he said he was particularly inspired by a line from "Reet Petite".

"Gypsy", with its strident acoustic guitar lines, pulled us back to a more familiar mellow tempo, but quickly switched into a powerful chorus section. The changing tempos flowed in and out of each other with amazing cohesion. Van had frequently professed much empathy for the gypsy and his way of life.

At first hearing "I Will Be There", accorded a thumping bar-room blues feel, might have seemed out of character, but on closer acquaintance, it emerged as a sort of subtle mood number with a pleasant lilt. Some delightful horn solos and more than a trace of the fifties blues artist, Joe Turner, were to be found.

"Listen to the Lion", of course, was one of the most memorable triumphs of this or any other Morrison album. It was a soaring exercise in effective rock dynamics. Chunky rhythm guitar, brushes whisking across the drum kit, trembling bongos, flat fat bass, chattering piano, dipping chords, topped off with a stunning vocal. Superlatives tear through the bloodstream. Van used his voice so superbly in this track that it seemed to become part of the instrumentation. A song of the power source, man unto himself. Van's schooling in the art of R & B repetition was never adapted so perfectly. The vocal zinged through the melody: altered inflections, delicate shading, a slight change in the lyric, over and over again, laying it down on top of you, implanting the message firmly in your mind. "Listen to the Lion" is Van Morrison to a V, miraculous energy funnelled through its ideal medium, dropping down on your head like a windfall of autumn leaves. At times it reaches such ecstatic heights that you feel like it's almost going to tear your head right off. Self-discovery unfolds before your vision.

"Listen to the Lion" and the title tune were to be the only tracks from *Saint Dominic's Preview* that he would continue performing live into 1974.

The second side opened in fine style too with the title song, full of flashing rhythms and imagery of Ireland and America. Vintage Van Morrison and a strong denunciation of absurd theories expounded in some rock magazines that the man was not an effective lyricist. Not to mention first class guitarwork.

"Redwood Tree" evoked memories of the carefree days of adolescence, the Belfast Cowboy growing up and finding his feet on home soil. A punchy and compassionate arrangement gave the track real bite, setting the stage for the arrival of the final song, "Almost Independence Day", the highlight of the album.

An extended essay in the stream-of-consciousness style, "Almost Independence Day" featured a sensitive and shimmering vocal, imaginative Moog background parts by Bernie Krause (who had previously performed on Simon and Garfunkel's "Save the Life of My Child" and "Space Odyssey" by the Byrds) and a staggering rapport among back-up musicians. Its meandering length and multi-images prompted some observers to draw comparisons with "Madame George". "It wasn't my concept to write a sequel to 'Madame George'," claims Morrison. "I like the song though. It was just contemplating organ and the Moog synthesizer. Everything was recorded live except that one high part on the synthesizer. I asked Bernie Krause to do this thing of China Town and then come in with the high part because I was thinking of dragons and fireworks. It reminded me of that. It was a stream-of-consciousness trip again."

Predictably there was an abundance of critical raves. "Morrison has a way of making spiritual statements," wrote *Creem* magazine's Dave Marsh, "that would sound either false or trite from almost anyone else, sound valid and refreshing. He has always, I think, dealt with a certain kind of spiritual regeneration, a type of self-discovery that is continually essential and essentially continual."

In *Rock Scene*, Daniel Goldberg stated: "*Saint Dominic's Preview* is a happy change for many of Van's fans. Rather than play it safe with a remake of *Tupelo Honey*, he has taken his entire range of past styles, added some new touches, and come up with his best album." *Rolling Stone*'s Stephen Holden felt it was the "best-produced, most ambitious Van Morrison yet released." He went on to note: ". . . above all *Saint Dominic's Preview* invokes the possibility of profound self-revelation through being on the road and making music." *Melody Maker* considered it "perhaps the first completely satisfying Van Morrison album since *Astral Weeks*, although they've all been great." *Zig Zag*'s long time Morrison freak John Tobler observed: ". . . I got the feeling I was hearing *the* album of 1972." The *Kentish Times* reported: ". . . magnificent, musically rich throughout although he never sticks to one style." And in *The Times*, Myles Palmer put it as bluntly as possible: "The cumulative impact is devastating."

Even Van Morrison was satisfied, more or less, with the

results. "The album was kind of rushed because of stupid things like studio time and stuff like that. But I thought it was a good shot, that album. There were a lot of good songs on it. *Saint Dominic's Preview* was more into where I'm at, more into what I was doing."

10 Looking down towards the light at the end of the tunnel: *Hard Nose the Highway* 1973

Van Morrison, November 1973: "The albums I connect up with are Astral Weeks, Moondance, Saint Dominic's Preview *and* Hard Nose the Highway. *They're the ones I like. But I've got a bad taste in my mouth for the* Street Choir *and* Tupelo Honey *albums.*"

By his own account, *Hard Nose the Highway* is the first album over which Morrison exercised complete artistic control and it can therefore be properly viewed as a thoroughly honest and personal work. Thus far it represented the least possible compromise which Morrison had to undergo in transmitting his work to the public at large. Even the recording sessions took place at Van's own studio located next door to his house in Fairfax, California. Bit by bit Van was gaining direction of his own musical destiny, but the old memories still burned on brightly.

"Seen some hard times,
Drawn some fine lines,
No time for shoe shines,
Hard Nose the Highway . . ."

"As a concept for the album," Van explained, "I was just trying to establish how hard it was to do just what I do. Plus there were some lighter things on the other side of it. One side has a kind of hard feeling while the other is soft. That's just about the concept of the album. I think that 'Wild Children' kind of stands out but I don't know . . . after listening to it, no one track stands out in particular."

Since *Hard Nose the Highway* represented a definite creative milestone for Morrison, it seems worthwhile to compare Van's personal viewpoints with the reactions of assorted rock critics. Although Morrison's expressed desire was to try and demonstrate through his music how difficult it was for him to produce such music to his personal satisfaction, the album contained several concurrent sub-themes: what many of his contemporaries were into as far as economic motivation was concerned; on the value of being one's own self; the immorality of hypocrisy; and the peculiar lives most of us have experienced in being the first and second generations to follow humanity's largest holocaust. In this last theme, virtually unexpressed in the annals of literature, Morrison placed the war children dilemma right on the line. He penetrated the sub-culture more deeply than any other musical artist that I can recall and with moving compassion.

Expressed as bluntly and coarsely as possible (and quoting from the headline of a review in an Irish daily) "Van Morrison gives childhood a big boost." But of course there was much more to it than that.

SNOW IN SAN ANSELMO

Snow in San Anselmo,
The deer cross by the lights,
The mission down in old San Rafael,
A madman looking for a fight.
A madman looking for a fight.

The massage parlor's open,
The clientele come and they go,
The classic music station,
Plays in the background soft and low.
Plays in the background soft and low.

The silence round the cascades,
The ice crisp and clear,
The beginning of the opera,
Seem to suddenly appear.
Seem to suddenly appear.

The pancake house is always crowded,
Open twenty-four hours of every day,
And if you suffer from insomnia,
You can speed your time away.
You can speed your time away.
Snow in San Anselmo,
My waitress my waitress my waitress
Said it was coming down,
Said it hasn't happened in over thirty years,
But it was laying on the ground.
But it was laying on the ground.

" 'Snow in San Anselmo'," says Van, "is a sketch on when it snowed in San Anselmo. It's about the images that were happening when it was snowing there for the first time in thirty years."

The song featured the soaring backing vocals of the Oakland Symphony Chamber Chorus. "A marvellous opening track," concluded *Melody Maker*'s Geoff Brown. Writing in the *Berkeley Barb*, Robert Blades said: "expertly produced and thoroughly enjoyable."

WARM LOVE

Look at the ivy on the old clinging wall,
Look at the flowers and the green grass so tall,
It's not a matter of when push comes to shove,
It's just an hour on the wings of a dove.

I dig it when you're fancy dressed up in lace,
I dig it when you have a smile on your face,
This inspiration's got to be on the flow,
This invitation's got to see it and know.

It's just Warm Love,
It's just Warm Love,

And it's everpresent everywhere,
And it's everpresent everywhere,
That Warm Love.

To the country I'm going,
Lay and laugh in the sun,
You can bring, bring your guitar along,
We'll sing some songs, we'll have some fun.
The sky is crying and it's time to go home,
And we shall hurry to the car from the foam,
Sit by the fire and dry out our wet clothes,
It's raining outside from the skies up above.

Inside it's Warm Love,
Inside it's Warm Love,
And it's everpresent everywhere,
And it's everpresent everywhere,
Warm Love, Warm Love.

" 'Warm Love' is just a boy and a girl song . . . walking on the beach. It's a young song," notes Van. "Warm Love" was a moderate Top 40 single hit and continues to be one of Morrison's most popular performance tunes. The catch line ". . . and it's everpresent everywhere, Warm Love . . ." was exceedingly engaging, one of Van's finest lyrical hooks in Top 40 terminology. "A smashing single" claimed *Melody Maker*, while *ZigZag*'s John Tobler heard it as "a second cousin to 'Crazy Love' and nearly as good."

HARD NOSE THE HIGHWAY

Hey kids dig the first takes,
Ain't that some interpretation,
When Sinatra sings against Nelson Riddle Strings,
Then takes a vacation.

Seen some hard times,
Drawn some fine lines,
No time for shoe shines,
Hard Nose the Highway.

I was tore down at the dead's place,
Shaved head at the organ,
But that wasn't half as bad as it was oh no,
In Belfast and Boston.

Put your money where your mouth is,
Then we can get something going,
In order to win you must be prepared to lose sometime,
And leave one or two cards showing.

"There's three things happening in 'Hard Nose the Highway'," says Van. "The first verse is an image of Frank Sinatra going in the studio and saying 'Let's do it.' He makes an album then walks out and takes a vacation. It's an image of professionalism. The second image is of Marin County. It's becoming more professional but it's a beautiful place. There are a lot of professionals there but the general attitude there is like this: if you take something into a shop to be fixed and they say come back in a week . . . and you come back in a week and they say: 'I dunno man, that won't be ready for two months.' Instead of telling you in the first place that they can't do it and suggesting you take it somewhere else. There's that kind of attitude in Marin County.

"The second verse is 'Tore down at the dead's place, Shaved head at the organ, But that wasn't half as bad as it was in Belfast and Boston' . . . that's kind of being weary with the scene. I'm not putting down anybody but I just can't get into that cult thing and that syndrome. The second verse is about being depressed but it doesn't matter because it doesn't make much difference anyway.

"The third verse is about record companies, promoters and all the business people in music . . . 'Put your money where your mouth is' and that's what that's about. The theme running through the whole song is 'Seen some hard times' which I have, 'Drawn some fine lines' which I definitely have, and 'No time for shoe shines' when you're trying to make a living. That's about the whole thing."

WILD CHILDREN

We were the War Children,
1945,
When all the soldiers came marching home,
Love looks in their eye.

Tennessee Tennessee Williams,
Let your inspiration flow,
Let it be around when we hear the sound,
When the spring time rivers flow, when the rivers flow.

Rod Steiger and Marlon Brando,
Standing with their heads bowed on the side,
Crying like a baby thinking about the time,
James Dean took that fatal ride, took that ride.

Tennessee Tennessee Tennessee,
Tennessee Williams,
Let your inspiration go,
Will you be around to hear the sound,
When the spring time rivers flow, rivers flow.

And Steiger and Marlon Brando,
Standing with their heads bowed on the side,
Crying like a baby thinking about the time,
James Dean took that fatal ride, took that ride.

And we were the Wild Children,
Back in 1945,
When all the soldiers came marching home,
Love looks love looks in their eyes, in their eyes.

"Wild Children", with its images of sub-culture idols of the silver screen such as actors James Dean, Marlon Brando and Rod Steiger along with the brilliant Southern playwright/ screenwriter, Tennessee Williams, is a perceptive statement about post-war adolescence. "For all of the kids born around that time," notes Van, "because of what it meant before that, I think there was a heavier trip to conform. For example, uniforms at school. I remember that one. Kids in the States never went through that, but we did. There's definitely been a whole break-through. I think that where that song is coming from is growing up in another country and getting our releases through figures from America, like the American anti-heroes. They were somebody representing something, that type of number. Whereas the kids coming up now are into a whole different thing: it seems a lot freer for one thing."

THE GREAT DECEPTION

Did you ever hear about The Great Deception,
Well the plastic revolutionaries take the money and run,
Have you ever been down to love city,
Where they rip you off with a smile,
And it don't take a gun.

Don't it hurt so bad in love city,
Don't it make you not want to bother at all,
And don't they look so self-righteous,
When they pin you up against the wall.

Did you ever, ever see the people.
With the tear drops in their eyes,
I just can't stand it, stand it no how,
Living in this world of lies.

Did you ever hear about the rock and roll singers,
Got three or four Cadillacs,
Saying power to the people, dance to the music,
Wants you to pat him on the back.

Have you ever heard about the great Rembrandt,
Have you ever heard about how he could paint,
And he didn't have enough money for his brushes,
And they thought it was rather quaint.

But you know it's no use repeating,
And you know it's no use to think about it,
'Cos when you stop to think about it,
You don't need it.

Have you ever heard about the great Hollywood motion
 picture actor,
Who knew more than they did,
And the newspapers didn't cover the story,
Just decided to keep it hid.

Somebody started saying it was an inside job,
Whatever happened to him,
Last time they saw him down on the Bow'ry,
With his lip hanging off an old rusty bottle of gin.

Have you heard about the so-called hippies,
Down on the far side of the tracks,
They take the eyeballs straight out of your head,
Say son, kid, do you want your eyeballs back.

With the teardrops in their eyes,
With the teardrops in their eyes,
Just can't stand it no how,
Living in this world of lies.

The hard side of "Hard Nose the Highway" closed on an epic note with "The Great Deception", one of the most stinging indictments from any observer, let alone a rock artist, of the tragic hypocrisy of so many participants in the sub-culture, in particular the big-time rock stars of this era.

"What inspired that song," says Van, "was that I met this revolutionary guy. I don't know how well known he was but he came on to me like he was interested in the scene. He may have been legitimate; maybe I'm putting him down for the wrong reason. But I just don't like people who write you a friendly letter and then halfway through the letter ask you for a large sum of money . . . after calling themselves revolutionaries. That's where the song started from."

Later Morrison told Steve Peacock of *Sounds*: "That song was for all the phonies." One verse related the tragic tale of a movie actor who was blackballed for annoying the moguls. "Hollywood," Van told Peacock, "is just another of the illusion trips. Fantasy trips that just fit into the deception. Like all those Hollywood movies making life out to be some kind of fairy tale. A lot of people in Hollywood are into their own scene, and believe their own publicity and stuff like that."

BEIN' GREEN
(Written by Joe Raposo)

It's not that easy Bein' Green,
Having to spend each day the color of the leaves,
When I think it could be nicer bein' red or yellow or gold,
Or something much more colorful like that.

It's not easy Bein' Green,
It seems you blend in with so many other ordinary things,
And people tend to pass you over,
'Cos you're not standing out like flashy sparkles,
On the water or stars in the sky.

But Green is the color of Spring,
And Green can be cool and friendly like,
And Green can be big like an ocean,
Or important like a mountain or tall like a tree.

When Green is all there is to be,
It could make you wonder why,
But why wonder, why wonder?
I am Green and it'll do fine, it's beautiful,
And I think it's what I want to be.

"Bein' Green", which opened side two, was the first non-original composition recorded by Morrison since joining Warner Brothers, and therefore deserves special attention. It was penned by one Joe Raposo, the major musical contributor to the outstanding U.S. children's TV series, Sesame Street, and was originally sung on the programme by Kermit the Frog.

" 'Bein' Green' of course is a song from Sesame Street," says Van, "but for me it has another meaning. That's why I thought I'd put it on this album. I think it's a good song for what it says about being green. That was just a statement that you don't have to be flamboyant. If somebody doesn't like you just because you're a certain thing, then maybe they're seeing the wrong thing. Maybe they're used to having everything flamboyant or everything uptempo so that they can't really see the real thing. That's what my interpretation is."

Not everybody was able to manage the mirage of the metaphor. An unidentified writer in the straight-laced British monthly *Records and Recording* (November 1973) said: ". . . even the kindest critic would call [it] a heap of slush." Little wonder that British children have yet to feel the thrill of a new kind of consciousness in kids' TV, if that review is any indication of local awareness (Sesame Street is not shown in the U.K. because it is considered too American-oriented!) *Zig-Zag*'s John Tobler concluded that "Green is the unifying factor of the record" while *Melody Maker* said: "Not a bad track . . . just strange." It strikes me as being an excellent rationale of Morrison's horror of static musical images as imposed by the media.

AUTUMN SONG

Leaves of brown they fall to the ground,
And it's here, over there leaves around,
Shut the door, dim the lights and relax,
What is more, your desire or the facts.

Pitter patter the rain falling down,
Little glamor sun coming round,
Take a walk when Autumn comes to town.

Little stroll past the house on the hill,
Some more coal on the fire will do well,
And in a week or two it'll be Hallowe'en,
Set the page and the stage for the scene.

Little game the children will play,
And as we watch them while time away,
Look at me and take your breath yeah.

You'll be smiling eyes beguiling,
And the song on the breeze,
Will call my name out and your dream.

Chestnuts roasting outside as you walk,
With your love by your side,
The old accordion man plays mellow and bright,
And you go home in the Christmas of the night.

Little later friends will be along,
And if you feel like joining the throng,
Just might feel like singing Autumn Song,
Just may feel like singing Autumn Song.

You'll be smiling eyes beguiling,
And the song on the breeze,
Calls my name out in your dream.

Chestnuts roasting outside,
As you walk with your love by your side,
And the old accordion man plays mellow and bright,
And you go home in the Christmas of the night.

The ten and a half minute "Autumn Song", Van claims, is "just an ode to autumn." The *Denver Post*'s Jared Johnson noted: "Van Morrison is a master at building moods. 'Autumn Song' is a prime example." I can't deny that it's the funkiest song about the splendors and moods of fall that has ever glided through my ears.

PURPLE HEATHER
(Traditional: Written by F. McPeake,
Re-arranged by Van Morrison).

Well the summer time has gone,
And the leaves are gently turning,
Yeah my love I wanna take,
To the place hot and yearning,
Where'll you go,
There she goes.

And we'll all go together,
In the wild mountain thyme,
All around the blooming heather,
Where'll you go.

And I will build my love a tower,
In the view of yonder mountain,
And live by the hour,
With the lily of the valley.
Where'd you go,
There she goes.

And we'll all go together,
In the wild mountain thyme,
All around the blooming heather,
Come on.

Hard Nose the Highway closed with "Purple Heather", another extended exercise in vocal dynamics. "'Purple Heather'," says Van, "is really 'Wild Mountain Thyme' . . . just my interpretation of 'Wild Mountain Thyme'. I like the arrangement of that. I really dig the way we did it: it worked out well I thought."

Generally the album enjoyed rave reviews but there's a doubting Thomas in every herd. Writing in the British magazine, *Let It Rock*, Charlie Gillett claimed: "The trouble with *Hard Nose the Highway* is that although the music is quite often interesting, it doesn't have a convincing emotional basis. The prevailing mood is of clean country air. Despite the lack of lyric inspiration and of melodic focus, the record is attractive to listen to. But Van Morrison has set high standards for himself and *Hard Nose the Highway* doesn't meet them."

The real sadness I suppose is that a tree had to be chopped down to provide the paper on which that review was printed. I would be ashamed to wrap my fish and chips in it.

For the purposes of recording this album, the Caledonia Soul Orchestra consisted of Jack Schroer and Jules Broussard (both veterans of *Saint Dominic's Preview*), Joseph Ellis and William Atwood on horns, guitarists John Platania and Van Morrison, Jef Labes on piano, drummers Gary Malabar and Rick Schlosser, David Hayes and Marty David on bass, and a string section led by Nathan Rubin with players Zaven Melikian, Nancy Ellis, Theresa Adams, John Tenny and Michael Gerling. *Hard Nose the Highway* was produced by Van Morrison for Caledonia Productions, Inc. with Jef Labes and Jack Schroer credited as Assistant Producers, and all three were listed as arrangers.

Jackie DeShannon (of "Needles and Pins", "What the World Needs Now", and "Put a Little Love in Your Heart" singles' fame) sang back-up vocals on "Warm Love" and the title song. This contribution and the fact that Miss DeShannon played some California gigs as an opening act for Van, prompted a few media types to link the pair romantically, in a sort of Kris Kristofferson–Rita Coolidge context. Morrison had also written and produced four tracks with Miss DeShannon for Atlantic Records. "I don't think anything was ever released . . . maybe they're holding them back or something," says Morrison.

"There never was a duet album planned," Van told one reporter in no uncertain fashion. "There was no team up. That whole thing was just the magazines talking. They write about something that they don't know anything about . . . just to make money. Something happens and they are sure it's worth bread, so they write it up. That's how those magazines exist."

Originally conceived as a double album, *Hard Nose the Highway* hit the marketplace in July 1973 as a remarkably cohesive album of outstanding music. The public could dig it too: Warner Brothers reported recently that the U.S. sales on this sixth Morrison album for the label were close to 200,000 units. Warner Brothers' president Joseph B. Smith was moved to comment: "On hearing some of Van's albums again, it was my feeling that we had the potential of a very important, long-lived artist should a lot of things break right."

Hard Nose the Highway was a significant step in the right direction; Van was now well into choosing his own path. It had taken six albums, but he was finally there. He had at last achieved artistic control over his own music and *Hard Nose the Highway* was an untarnished indicator of what one might reasonably expect from his future.

11 Unlocking the myths of a timid, tipsy gypsy of sorts, and a real live triumph: *It's To Late to Stop Now* 1973–1974

Van Morrison is a long-time believer in the inherent benefits of recording live with, and before, an audience. He had frequently claimed that the only way Them could have been captured effectively on record was on stage at the Maritime Hotel in Belfast and the actual sessions which took place in London recording studios were not much more than an artistic sham. And as far back as *Moondance*, he was expressing his opinion that the ideal method of producing music was in front of a live audience.

Yet there was an ironic paradox at work here. While Morrison believed implicitly that the presence of an audience enhanced his own performance, his own reputation implied otherwise or so it seemed. It had become difficult for some people to see beyond the mound of myths. It was a regular occurrence to hear vast discourses on Van's live gigs by people who had never seen the man work on stage. As a result, it was widely believed that Morrison was an alcoholic, a dope addict (this was a particularly frequent claim since it was felt that no artist could create such powerfully emotional music without drugs), given to falling off stages in his drunken stupor, a timid tipsy gypsy of sorts. It was assumed that Van Morrison was at best an erratic and unwilling live performer, a reluctant artist whose only real playing power was exhibited in the recording studio.

Nothing could have been further from the truth. In the case of Van Morrison however, the media and the public have seldom allowed the truth to get in the way of the thrills of intrigue, absorbing what it felt good to believe. As it happened, Van was seldom satisfied with the staging and organization of his concerts, and with his pursuit of perfection he frequently found himself being distracted by annoying details. Managers, agents and gig promoters were obsessed with counting ticket takings; because Van's feelings about the conduct of his appearances had little to do with the dollar gross, they were generally ignored, with the inevitable result that Morrison was often unable to put his mind into simply making his music. Few of the people involved in packaging his concerts were able to draw the distinction between an artist and an entertainer; they did not have the sensitivity or creative empathy to appreciate Morrison's dilemma. They did not speak his language.

What's with this little schmuck, coming on with all this crap about no spotlights, no pop star trips, wants to play from down in the front row or something, down with the people? Who the hell does he think he is? What promoter is going to put up with any goddam conditions for some dude who doesn't even have a record in the top ten? He should realize how lucky he is to be able to play any damn concerts already. The nerve of these goddam kids.

It wasn't until the latter part of 1973, when it was possible for Van to create satisfactory conditions at his concerts, that he finally emerged as one of the most potent live performers on the contemporary scene. This aspect of his career will be dealt with in considerable detail shortly; it will suffice at this point to assert the fact that Van Morrison's entire attitude to live performances has undergone a vast change in the past year or so.

And so it followed that his new confidence in the concert sphere – and his intuitions about the inherent benefits of cutting records in the more natural atmosphere of the performing stage – should soon be manifested in the recording of a live album. A double LP set entitled *It's Too Late to Stop Now* was released by Warner Brothers in February 1974.

"The album is basically a re-statement," Van observed a few weeks prior to the release. "It's just that a lot of these songs, I think, come off better live. They're different anyway, when done live. It represents, and is in context, with what I do performing as far as the overall picture of the album is concerned. I don't necessarily want to make albums much closer to what I'm doing on stage. That's the dilemma: it's really hard. I do the mellow stuff and I do the harder stuff and I do a lot of other stuff. It doesn't throw the audience off, but it's kind of hard to please everybody.

"That's what I've been finding in the performances . . . they get off and all that but there's so many different types of people who dig my music, so it's hard to make a record. Some people want to hear this album, some people want to hear another album. So this new album represents what we did live on the Fall 1973 tour. Basically it's interpretations of the songs: a lot of them are better than my original records, better than what's been out before. Songs do mature with age, I think.

"The 'Wild Children' track that we recorded live is a killer, it's much better than the version on *Hard Nose the Highway*. When we recorded that song, we weren't really into it. I'd just written the tune then we went straight in and recorded it. Ideally you should take a song on the road for a couple of months and live with it a while. That would be the best time to record it, I believe. *It's Too Late to Stop Now* includes my own songs such as 'Caravan', 'Domino', 'Into the Mystic', 'Warm Love', 'These Dreams of You', 'Listen to the Lion' and 'Saint Dominic's Preview', plus a bunch of other songs that I like but didn't write: things like Bobby Blue Bland's 'Ain't Nothing You Can Do'; Ray Charles' 'I Believe To My Soul'; 'Help Me', the Sonny Boy Williamson tune; Sam Cooke's 'Bring It On Home To Me'; Willie Dixon's 'I Just Wanna Make Love To You'; and 'Take Your Hand Out of My Pocket' by Sonny Boy Williamson."

One wondered if this new-found exuberance for live performing might influence Van into joining the multitudes of rock bands tramping around America on unending weeks of dollar-harvesting one-nighters and, indeed, precisely when his personal turnaround had taken place. "I think it would be suicide for me to perform the whole year around," he said emphatically. "But I am getting more into performing. It's incredible. When I played Carnegie Hall in New York in the Fall (1973) something just happened. All of a sudden I felt like 'you're back into performing' and it just happened like that. Click. I was just standing on the stage and I was singing and it just hit me, I was back into performing. A lot of times in the past I've done gigs and it was rough to get through them. But now the combination seems to be right and it's been clicking a lot."

With the live album, Morrison's rigid concept from the start was that, unlike most live rock LP's, no studio overdubbing and patching up would take place after the fact, and that any tracks released would be absolutely authentic to the performance. This explains the absence of "Moondance" from the live album. Van originally planned to use the song, but one wrong guitar note prevented its inclusion. He would not permit the over-dubbing of a mere one note of music. "Van has a sense of black and white about things like this," explained Stephen Pillster, Van's business representative at the time. "He would not overdub one note or anything. So it really was an absolutely honest live album, perhaps the first ever."

It was also one of the first live albums to incorporate string players. In the early spring of 1973, Morrison had tested out a string section in a three-day stint at the Troubador club in Los Angeles. The section was led by first violin player of the Oakland Symphony Orchestra, Nathan Rubin, and Van's road manager Ron Gibson stated: "Van has been waiting to use strings onstage for some time and these were exactly the guys he was looking for." The string section comprised violinists Tim Kovatch, Tom Halpin and Nancy Ellis, celloist Terry Adams and Rubin.

The rhythm unit of the Caledonia Soul Orchestra included Jeff Labes on piano and organ (he also wrote the first-class string arrangements), drummer Dahaud Shaar, John Platania on guitar, and bassist David Hayes, along with Jack Schroer on saxes and Bill Atwood on trumpet. These ten musicians represented a truly top notch combination, probably the most talented that Van had worked with up until this point. By the time the autumn 1973 tour rolled out of San Francisco, Morrison felt that the Caledonia Soul Orchestra was the best band he'd had in years. At last things were beginning to cook, his Carnegie Hall revelations were just a few sets away. Van was convinced of his readiness to put down on tape some of the gigs for the live album. Concerts at three separate venues – The Troubador in Los Angeles, Santa Monica's Civic Auditorium and the Rainbow Theatre in London – were recorded and the finished album comprised segments of each of these appearances.

Audience reaction to the performances was at an all-time high and Van responded accordingly. In *Playgirl* magazine Marco Baria described the Troubador gig: ". . . he was exceptional. The mood was right, the audience was receptive, and the music left no comparisons to be made. It was the finest opening night performance by a consummate musician that I have ever witnessed."

The two Rainbow concerts in London represented Morrison's first appearance in the city since the days of Them some six years earlier. The critical consensus was that the performances were *the* rock event of the year. *Record Mirror*'s Peter Harvey said that Van had "*The* voice of rock 'n' roll.' Myles Palmer of *The Times* concluded: "Here for once was a concert about which one could cast aside all reservations. It demolished all barriers between the soul, blues, jazz and rock genres. The ensemble playing of his 10-piece Caledonia Soul Orchestra was simply the most sophisticated and unusual I have heard in a decade of continuous exposure to pop performances."

The Financial Times' Antony Thorncroft noted: "Van Morrison has enough control and experience to win through where Joe Cocker, perhaps his closest competitor as a white urban blues singer fell away." Robin Denselow of *The Guardian* said: "It was a tense, thrilling and emotional night, for in the time he has been away, Van Morrison has become arguably the finest white blues singer in the world." And the *Evening Standard*'s Andrew Bailey described the Raibow atmosphere: "His appearance was preceded by an air of expectancy as heavy as that before a performance by Olivier or Nureyev."

Fortunately these emotion-packed moments were monumentally preserved in the grooves of *It's Too Late To Stop Now*, the phrase which Van had traditionally used to close off a live performance. Six months after its release, Warner Brothers reported the album had sold "well over 100,000 copies and is still selling consistently and will probably be up in the higher figures within the next few months." It was a brilliantly-conceived reversal by an artist who had been all but written off as a concert performer. Always a staunch believer in the spontaneity and honesty of recording in the performing context, Morrison had pulled off one of the finest live albums in rock history. It was an outstanding recapitulation of Morrison's first fifteen years as a musical artist, composer and performer, a real triumph for a man who'd had to fight every inch of the way to preserve the purity of his music. He'd won – and really it was more a case of it being too early to stop yet.

12 Getting the chaff out of the harvesting machine and feeding the lions: Unauthorized albums 1963–1968

Van Morrison, I think you will agree, has been subjected to more than his share of music industry rip-offs. Over the years there has been no shortage of low-class (quick buck) individuals clamouring for a chance to turn his name into a money-making machine, to steer him into the rock star pastures where the pickings were much more plentiful. They'd have sold his soul for a dollar, as long as they were guaranteed their ten per cent. They all knew that Morrison had what it takes to succeed, their problem was only in convincing him to take the conventional road to rock stardom. Doesn't everybody want to be rich, to be famous, to be a subject of envy? What else would a kid possibly want? It's the American Dream come true and didn't Morrison come to America to join the Dream? Accustomed to dealing with acts whose only concern was how much they could earn for the minimum effort, the industry leeches could not cope with the possibility that Van Morrison might be an artist primarily motivated by his art, a person who actually had a semblance of moral worth. Christ, only some doped-out musician would possibly want to make music for music's sake.

Morrison's unbending attitudes and his fierce conviction about his music was probably the major reason why so many people were reluctant to allow him creative freedom. Why, he might be dangerous to the health of the industry, somehow he might dampen the dollar flow. That would be high treason and was to be prevented at all cost.

In retrospect, the cost was to be the enforced reduction of Van's creative flow. If this kid was going to be part of their industry, then they'd damn well make sure that he did things their way. It might well be pertinent to point out at this stage that the music industry had traditionally operated on the premise that the actual musicians and composers should have as little creative control in the production and marketing of their music as legally possible. So what if the artist has little say in what is pushed at the public in his or her name, it's the company that puts up the money in the first place that gets to call the shots. Admittedly there have been some drastic changes in this routine in more recent times but these refinements literally were forced down the industry's throat at no little cost. Very few aspects of creative control have been handed over to the creators without bitter and prolonged contract negotiation.

Van Morrison's career is a supreme example of such contentions. If ever there was a single artist whose artistic strength was so obvious and who therefore had such an absolute right to direct every phase of his music, it was Morrison. Composer-lyricist-poet-arranger-producer-musician-singer, he was a master in every category but still they would not pass over the creative reins.

Right from Them's beginnings until the *Saint Dominic's Preview* album, Van swears he was not permitted the final say in the presentation of his music . . . a period which saw the recording of such genuine rock classics as "Gloria", "Brown Eyed Girl", "T. B. Sheets", "Cypress Avenue", "Madame George", "Moondance", "Caravan" and "Brand New Day".

Producers had the audacity to tell him *how* to sing at Them recording sessions, and he was bitterly dissatisfied with the results. Bang Records, he claims, persuaded him to record a bunch of singles which were then released in the unacceptable form of two albums. His words are not totally without malice when he describes the second of these albums, *The Best of Van Morrison* as "more like The Worst of Van Morrison." Signed to Warner Brothers through the independent production company Schwaid/Merenstein, he says he was not allowed to suggest session musicians, track selection and order, or jacket artwork. He was in short the tool of people anxious to get a product onto the shelves. It might be partly his music, but it was their money. Art and money are seldom a splendid pairing.

In addition to such dubious productions, two separate albums have been released (one each by Bang and Decca/Parrot) which Morrison publicly declared to be without his knowledge or approval. It may not be pointless to note that record buyers would be serving the honourable cause of artistic integrity by questioning the real value of these albums. I must say that there is something inherently abominable about record companies which would seek to blight an artist's name and career by issuing music which does not have the blessing of its creator. The artist is forced to live with such afflictions forever.

In 1973, Bang released an album entitled *T. B. Sheets* which comprised tracks from *Blowin' Your Mind* and *The Best [Worst] of Van Morrison*, along with rejected tracks from the same sessions, including "Madame George" and "Beside You", both of which appeared, after extensive negotiation by Warner Brothers, on the *Astral Weeks* album. Morrison says that he approached Bang for permission to remix the tracks before they were re-issued; but he did not receive even the courtesy of a reply.

Decca/Parrot weren't far behind in trying to cash in on the acceptance of Morrison's Warner Brothers albums. 1973 saw the release of a double album *Them Featuring Van Morrison Lead Singer*, which was basically a compilation of *Them* and *Them Again*, plus a couple of previous rejects. Few of the cuts actually featured the group Them and many of the backing tracks came from studio musicians. Morrison was treated at these sessions as little more than a puppet, to be manipulated by a myriad of producers who neither knew nor cared in the slightest what the artist might desire. The artistic value of such productions was indeed questionable.

What this seemed to represent, in the view of *Reliable Sources*, Morrison's media information kit distributed in the spring of 1974, was expressed thus: "It's yet another justification for Van's belief that the music business is for reasons other than music."

13 The frustrations and struggles of the existential performer: Live performances

Of late, more and more people have begun to believe that Van Morrison has become the most compelling and charismatic performer in rock music of the seventies. When he's on, his concerts, like his music, climb to unprecedented emotional heights. By the most subtle means, he can achieve a stark dramatic effect of a depth unknown to the theatrically-oriented performers of rock: the Bowies, Coopers and Dolls. His elusiveness and his obvious disdain for anything other than simply making his music can make his concerts absolutely electrifying. His shunning of the usual egotistical effects at rock concerts – the spotlights, the fashionable glamour, outlandish self-adornment – his obsessive desire to strip away all of the superfluous frills of nonsense entertainment, his lingering introversion in public: Van Morrison surely represents the antithesis of the contemporary rock star. Yet, by simply doing what he believes he must do and ignoring what the industry told him he should do, I think Van Morrison let loose on the concert stage can unleash an emotional potency unknown to the likes of Mick Jagger, Elvis Presley and Robert Plant.

If any individual had doubts about the legitimacy of this music as an enduring art form, they only have to attend a Van Morrison concert to be convinced that his music is as serious and as valid as any performance of Brahms, Schubert or Mozart. The times may have changed and the medium may be different, but the message remains the same.

This is a truly remarkable turnaround for an artist who was considered by many to be a lame duck performer up until a year or so ago. The crux of the matter is that Morrison was not a performing entertainer in the accepted sense. His gigs were either performed on his own terms or they didn't come off; and it wasn't until recently that critics were prepared to judge him on those terms. You could not, for instance, impose the yardsticks on Morrison that one would apply to Cat Stevens, Elton John, John Denver or even George Harrison. Yet the media has to a degree been guilty of such shortsightedness in Morrison's regard: it's a sad situation that elements in the media have often had immense difficulty in simply accepting an artist as he is and for what he is.

Nevertheless it must be admitted that his performing career, prior to 1973, had its share of ups and downs. Long-time enthusiasts of his music recall, with a certain warped fondness, those nights when Van was damn near plastered out of his skull on booze, barely able to recall the lyrics to his songs, as he reeled and rocked. When things weren't right, literally everything went wrong. On some occasions, Van became enraged by the ineptitude of one or more of his backing musicians and on at least one evening (at San Francisco's Winterland Ballroom before 6,000 people in November 1971) he actually stalked off the stage, angry not at the audience but at his own band.

He'd been really down at the time – depressed by the music business and its lack of compassion for artistic integrity. No one could care less about an artist endeavouring to faithfully create his art before live audiences. He was mid-way through what one might rather delicately term his performing paranoia period. A series of misfortunes and management misdemeanours had prevented him from performing in the manner in which he felt his music must be presented. And it really dragged his ass. It actually made him afraid to get out on the stage and it was little wonder he sought liquid refuge from these fears.

People who had seen Van perform in Them's triumphant days at the Maritime Hotel in Belfast would have been amazed at his subsequent reticence to bop around in berserk fashion upon the concert stage. During that period Morrison was an extroverted rock 'n' roller, given to cutting loose with the wildest of his contemporaries. Singer Dave Mason who witnessed several Them gigs in England, recalls that Van was "crazy" on stage. Mason says he would jump around the stage and leap up on speaker cabinets and often sounded "pretty incoherent". It may have had something to do with Van's inability to take Them seriously once they'd departed the Maritime Hotel stage.

This was a passing phase. Around the time that *Astral Weeks* was released (late 1968) Van adopted a more personal and natural style which he continues to maintain. All of his solo material for Bang Records was recorded with session musicians and the first performing group he put together in America consisted of guitarist Charlie Brown, drummer Bob Grenier and

Eric Oxendine on bass. A few months prior to the recording of *Astral Weeks*, he formed an unusual trio comprising John Payne on flute, Tim Kilbania on upright bass and himself. This combination completed one East Coast tour which was not especially successful and disbanded shortly thereafter. In the summer of 1969, Van assembled a new six-piece group featuring a horn section which has been his basic working line-up until now, albeit with various personnel changes along the way.

It has always been a chronic problem for Van to find the right sort of musicians, not only with a suitable temperament, but also an ability to play more than the basic three-chord rock 'n' roll repertoire. Such difficulties have plagued him right up to the present and they compounded his paranoia about performing.

In 1971 he was ready to admit that performing had become a "pretty agonizing" experience. It was not unlikely that he would "almost withdraw" a few minutes before he was expected on stage and it often took a full four numbers before he felt at ease in the concert environment.

The basic rock concert formula generally consists of recreating the hit singles and better known album tracks as close as possible to the original recorded sound, the traditional rock 'n' roll standard to confirm roots, a drum solo to prove instrumental ability; the whole mix to be delivered to the audience with a pelvic thrust and massive volume. Morrison has never filled that bill. He's just not in that space at all. From the top, he has never been able to perform in puppet fashion, churning out the songs note for note to the records. "I just can't sing any song the same way twice," Van insists. With each performance, he strives to create something new and fresh; the last thing he wants to do is recreate a memory from the past, a neat little repackaging of a feeling which only existed in a brief space of time. There is immense difference between the commonplace method and the Morrison approach.

"For me, performing requires a tremendous amount of concentration," he once confessed. "I'm not someone who just plugs in and gets it on. And it's hard to get audiences to listen because they're used to people who get it on. And that's just not what I do. Also I never do a song the same way twice. And of course the audiences always want to hear the old songs. They don't realize that when we used to do 'Gloria', for example, it was twenty minutes long and, on the record, it was only three minutes.

How are you going to recreate something like that? Anyway I get tired of being on the road after a while. Sometimes it's more important to do an album to get new songs out."

Another hassle for Morrison was his strong preference for an intimate concert atmosphere. This word "intimate" has been mashed out of any real meaning by the cliché merchants and it would be well to draw some distinctions. The word has been bandied around by acts such as Neil Young, Carole King and Bob Dylan, yet most of them have long since succumbed to the greatly-extended personal revenues to be drawn from acoustically-inferior stadiums, arenas and coliseums. There is a drastic shortage of concert halls in North America and Europe capable of seating in excess of 5,000 people. The limp excuse for playing in sports venues, as offered by a multitude of top rock acts, is that their following is so large in numerical quantity that it would be improper to impose attendance restrictions by appearing in the smaller locations. Dare one suggest that such ragged rationale is just shuck and jive to disguise the real motives? Might one be frivolous enough to put forth for your consideration a couple of reasonable alternatives? If indeed an act's potential audience is so huge that it requires a 20,000 seat capacity, then why not play five nights at a 4,000 seat concert hall where the sound quality has definite possibilities? Or, if the appropriate concert hall cannot be located and the only availability is a giant stadium, why not reduce the ticket prices (say from $6 to $2) to compensate for the loss in sound and vision inevitably experienced in such non-musical environments? Being well aware of the moral and monetary standards of many top rock entertainers, one does not anticipate any sudden rush to comply with my suggestions; but I must say that I can find no justification whatsoever for any act receiving in excess of $100,000 for a single live performance and I don't care if the act is offering an Andy Warhol movie backdrop, a David Bailey slide show, outstanding light effects, a battery of Moog synthesizers, free downers or violet velvet jock straps.

It pleases one immensely therefore to note that Van Morrison is not about to join the ranks of big-bread bonanza gig headliners; once again he is a glorious exception. "The thing is that I'm not an entertainer," Van told Roy Carr of the *New Musical Express* in the autumn of 1973. "I'm an artist, a musician . . . and there's a great difference. The difference between being an artist and an entertainer is that most rock 'n' roll acts are primarily entertainers. The music is relegated to secondary importance. If you play the big stadiums, like most bands feel compelled to, you put yourself in great danger of losing contact with a large percentage of your audience. I went to see a few groups in the summer, and it was only those people who were right down the front who were giving off any positive energy.

"Those people in the audience who were around the perimeter couldn't really have cared less if a group was up there on stage or not. They were either too stoned or they'd just come along because somebody told them it was the hip thing to do. Like there were 25,000 people who turned up at one event I went to, and well over half of them didn't see or hear a thing that was going on. I prefer a much more intimate surrounding. To tell you the truth, I wish I could work clubs but with a band of my present size, it's not economical. I wouldn't even break even."

It is advisable to underline these statements with the important fact that Morrison does not lack the legion of fans required to fill up sports stadiums; and indeed he has had a surfeit of offers from this direction. It is merely that he does not feel he could perform with satisfactory quality and intimacy in these circumstances. And we're back once again with that unhip old word, integrity. His kind of honesty and dedication could bear much imitation by his rock contemporaries. It would undoubtedly make the entire scene a great deal more enjoyable for us all. It's been a long, long time coming, and that in itself is a rather sad commentary on the current state of creative endeavour in rock music.

In 1973, despite the assorted myths which had built up about his varying standard of live performance, Morrison instituted the boldest move in his concert career. He put together a ten-piece band, the Caledonia Soul Orchestra, and incorporated a strong section "borrowed" from the Oakland Symphony Orchestra and led by Nathan Rubin. The tour kicked off in the late summer and wound its way around most big North American cities before jetting across the Atlantic to Europe where Morrison had not appeared since the Them period of 1964–66. The Caledonia Soul Orchestra consisted of some familiar faces, including Jeff Labes on keyboards, drummer Dahaud Shaar, John Platania on guitar, sax player Jack Schroer, Bill Atwood on trumpet and a new bass player, David Hayes, recruited from the ranks of Jesse Colin Young's band. The string section comprised Nathan Rubin on first violin, Tom Kovacs, Nancy Ellis on viola and Terry Adams on cello. The combination felt good right from the start and Morrison wasn't long in deciding to fulfil his dreams of a live album.

By the time Van and the Caledonia Soul Orchestra thundered into New York's Carnegie Hall, Morrison became aware that after several years of frustration in his stage work, the trip had clicked back into place. Gone were the nerves, the neurotic attacks of stage fright, the nightly fit of post-gig depression. Christ, he was actually enjoying himself out there, getting off as it were on the joyful vibes of well-organized presentation and a band that was really cooking, not to mention the ecstatic audience reaction. This newly-discovered (or recovered) enthusiasm could only mean one thing: his concerts were climbing from strength to strength. The European engagements, in particular, were a spectacular success. The British music press was solidly boosting his long-awaited arrival in London with extraordinary vigour, the scene was set for a literal avalanche of acclaim. This was to be no mere English rainshower, it was a full-scale tropical hurricane.

Roy Carr of the *New Musical Express* flew to Amsterdam to catch the opening continental performance while *Melody Maker*'s Michael Watts filed a piece from New York. "I've seen Presley in Vegas," wrote an enraptured Roy Carr, "James Brown at the Apollo and I guess what's generally considered to be the best of the rest. And last Thursday evening, I bore witness to what I can only describe as a most incredible non-performance from Van Morrison at the Carre Theatre in Amsterdam and he won hands down. It was no contest. But damn it, the man hardly moved on stage. I have to own up, I've never seen anything quite like it before, or for that matter have I been so enthralled by such a premeditated lack of visual entertainment."

Melody Maker's Michael Watts reported: "Morrison is essentially a craftsman rather than a showman, avoiding even eye-contact with his audience and allowing them the luxury of few spoken words. That he achieves such a ridiculous empathy with them is due less to any outward show of personality than to the power of his music and the perfectly judged way in which he wields it: always building, cutting instantly from one song to another and performing without a trace of excess until the emotions are milked and squeezed to a head. Perhaps, all said and done, he's the ultimate showman. He's become I think the best white blues singer of them all in a style or tradition that has more to do with the jazz feel of the fifties than the rock 'n' roll inflection of the sixties." Van supports this latter contention.

Thus the British music critics, freqently more perceptive than their American counterparts, had sussed out some of the reasons behind Morrison's rediscovery of his performing talent. Van was simply being himself and finally the rock scene – jaded perhaps by a stream of low musical content glitter and pseudo-glamour acts – was ready to accept it. Even before Morrison set foot on the Rainbow theatre stage in London, most members of the audience were absolutely convinced they were about to witness the highlight of the musical year. It could be no other way. And it was to be a triumph of music for music's sake, a connection with an infinitely-greater reason for the existence of this music than the recent infatuation with tits and ass. Shit-kicking can be fun but it's nice to get up to real purity now and again. And Van Morrison provided the archway.

The only allegedly souring note of the European tour was Van's decision to pass over playing in Ireland. Predictably there were extenuating circumstances. Nevertheless the fact that it was now more than seven years since he had set foot in his homeland, let alone performed there, and his several appearances in the British vicinity seemed to be too much for some Irish followers to swallow. The prevailing disillusionment was brought to the veritable boil by an incorrect announcement on the BBC TV programme The Old Grey Whistle Test to the effect that Van definitely would perform in Dublin at the end of the current tour. The controversy sparked by conflicting stories forced Van to issue a special statement explaining the circumstances and indicating that he planned to return to play in Ireland in the spring of 1974. Even this did not appear to placate wounded Irish souls. The Irish correspondent for *New Musical Express*, Colin McClelland, explained: "Can you understand how we feel over here when a guy we all knew around the pubs and at corners, who we haven't seen for seven years, who we can't really believe is the same bloke on the cover of all those albums everybody's buying all over the world, who comes to Britain without paying us a call, who suddenly, unbelievably, incredibly, changes his mind, decides he can't make it atfer all. How do you just stand up a whole nation?"

"I'm caught one more time up on Cypress Avenue."

The mystical, magical Van Morrison, caught one more time and just a hundred miles south of Cypress Avenue. Home again (or as close as anyone could reasonably expect him to get, considering the current circumstances of his homeland) to perform for the Irish folk who shared his experience of growing up in the fifties upon the emerald isle. Caught for the first time in eight years on a concert stage in Ireland; and for the first time ever as the lad from Belfast who became one of the handful of genuinely-gifted singer/songwriters who have turned on the world in the seventies. In a sense, you might say that Van Morrison escaped and triumphed.

By any other name it is a homecoming with all that that entails. Ireland's most precious gift to the international rock music scene (and indeed, to the contemporary literary scene at large) returns to play before his homeland. Rock music has become the ultimate medium of youthful communication in the electronic age; Van Morrison is very likely the modern day James Joyce. And eight years is a long, long time in a country whose very soul lies shattered in the ghettos and cemeteries of Belfast. The grim reaper has had a field day.

Let's set this record straight right from the outset: it certainly wasn't planned for Morrison to open this 1974 European tour in Dublin. He and his Caledonia Soul Express had left the States on 17 March after a stupendous three-encore performance at the Capitol Theatre in Passaic, N.J. In the words of Stephen Pillster, then general manager of Van's Caledonia Productions Inc.: "We had a certain momentum happening coming out of the States and everyone was really looking forward to those British dates. Then a day after we arrived, Van came down with the 'flu and a 104 degree fever, and we had no choice but to cancel out the first few dates."

The cancellation affected two sold-out gigs at London's Edmonton Sundown, plus concerts in Bristol, Manchester,

Cyprus Avenue, Belfast, scene of deep youthful inspiration

Northern Ireland Tourist Board

Memories of Belfast's Maritime Hotel remain, but now the building is used solely by the British Sailors' Society

Fitzroy Avenue out of 'Madame George'

Northern Ireland Tourist Board

Van Morrison's first performance in Ireland since 1966: The Olympic Theatre in Dublin, March 1974

An ailing Van Morrison on stage at the Olympic Theatre in Dublin, March 1974

Ritchie Yorke

In 1974, Van resumed playing auto saxophone at gigs: The Olympia Theatre, Dublin, March 1974

Glasgow and Birmingham. Other dates in Dublin, Paris, Brussels, Copenhagen and Amsterdam were, at that time, in definite jeopardy.

Many other money-motivated artists would simply have packed up the band and sent them back home to California, cancelled the entire tour and announced plans of a return at a later date. That was the easiest way out and economically it would have been the obvious move, not to mention the man's traditional dislike of being on the road. A swarm of recent concert cancellations in the U.K. had not helped matters, and *New Musical Express*, the weekly rock paper, felt moved to reprint the official signed medical certificate on its front page:

> "This is to certify that I was called in to see Mr. Van Morrison, on the 21st March, 1974, when he had collapsed and retired to bed with a high fever. This man had had a previous bout of fever when in Hawaii, three weeks previously. He had probably returned to full activity before he was properly cured at that time, and has now had a severe relapse with the same virus. His condition was the same today with high fever and a respiratory disease. In my opinion he will not be able to resume his occupation for several days."
>
> Signed, Dr. F. J. Hughes, MRCS, LRCP.

Whatever his personal feelings about the joys and traumas of live performance, Van Morrison ain't the sort of guy who light-heartedly pikes out on playing when people are expecting him. As we are going to witness during this Dublin weekend, Morrison is a true professional dedicated to the ancient artistic adage that the "show must go on."

The foundations for these homecoming gigs in Dublin were laid back in October when Van and his lady had taken a three week holiday in Ireland, his first time home in some seven years. He was approached by the organizers of Dublin Music Week '74, an affair which the promoter and his sponsor, the brewers of Bass beer, were hoping to turn into an annual event. Van had been in good spirits and was in the midst of writing a batch of new songs for his *Veedon Fleece* album. The promoters hit on him at the right time and Stephen Pillster, busily putting the background pieces together in Caledonia Productions' home office in San Rafael, California, suddenly received a call from

Van asking him to fly over to handle the arrangements. When Pillster flew in to Dublin a couple of days later, the elusive Mr. Morrison and his lady had departed on a motoring tour of the island.

The Morrison dates were confirmed (two concerts on both 30 and 31 March) and the remainder of Dublin Music Week would include shows by the Chieftains, Humphrey Lyttleton and Ronnie Scott, Tim Hardin, German classical/singer Veronica Jochum, and Elmer Bernstein conducting the RTESO, the local broadcasting media orchestra.

Dublin's Olympia Theatre, by any reckoning, is an amazing hall, truly a stunning relic of a fast-vanishing age. Originally called the Star Theatre of Varieties, it was built by a Mr. Dan Lowery in 1879 in Crampton Court, just off Dame Street, with the rear section of the building planted firmly astride the River Poddle. It was renamed the Olympia in 1922 when the new Irish government assumed control.

In the grim days of the thirties, Dubliners found comic relief in the Mrs. Bernard Shaw-sponsored production of a play about syphilis called *Brieux's Damaged Goods*, translated from the French. Some comment on the conflicting ideals of that era can be found in the fact that although the live production was drawing packed houses, the text of the play was totally banned in bookstores.

The arival of mass-media home entertainment through the tube contributed to the deterioration of the old musical hall during the fifties. The four walls and the land (and river presumably) beneath the Olympia were seized by property speculators in the early sixties and only the decisive intervention of the present management (which happened to own the theatrical contents of the hall) saved it from inevitable destruction by the wreckers' ball. Since 1964, the Olympia has mainly presented theatrical and "serious" music productions and we are told that tonight's performance is the first real rock concert ever to have taken place here.

A local historian describes the Olympia entrance as consisting of a "rococo canopy", such dull-sounding words for something so thoroughly beautiful. It is all milky glass and swirling iron lattice work, carved cherubs bearing flaming torches and bunches of grapes, gilded ceilings and gas lamps – such a charming change from the mass-made moronity of the plastic age.

The hall has a capacity of 1,400, scattered through two balconies, the stalls and half a doxen boxes on each side of the stage. There's a certain Shakespearian feel to the rich red velvet curtains and the miniature gold-painted, silk-tasseled lamps. You just know that without the concrete (deadly for echo) and mountains of space which destroy the soul of many concert arenas, rock 'n' roll is gonna sound real good in here tonight. The Olympia is about as close as one can get to the ideal, intimate rock venue.

Dublin is somewhat off the beaten rock path. Concerts are few and far between. The only posters you see daubed around town are for upcoming gigs by Neil Sedaka (making a comeback through Britain) and James Last, the German bandleader. Rory Gallagher, an Irishman himself, plays here occasionally. Ralph McTell was a recent visitor and Led Zeppelin and Focus have dropped in over the past year. People still talk heatedly about last year's gigs, especially at Dublin's rather seamy Revolution discothèque which members of Zep allegedly wrecked during their one and only trip across the sea to Ireland.

All four Van Morrison concerts have been sold out well in advance and there are early reports of busloads of Belfasters on the highway heading south.

There are four of us booked in at the once-plush Shelbourne Hotel, just across the road from Saint Stephen's Green, a sedate park with a pond where the carcase of some poor dead duck drifts, its head under the stagnant water, for three whole days as passers-by wonder how come a duck can keep its head underwater for so long. Down in the Constitution Room (so named because the room was the location of the drafting of the Constitution for the Irish Free State in 1922), the Shelbourne's chef, Maurice O'Looney, supervises the serving of hundreds of plates of plaice and chips to the assembled convention multitudes. After all it is Friday.

We four – a journalist and a photographer from *Melody Maker*, a Warner Brothers representative, and myself – settle in the Horseshoe Bar and toast our good fortune to be present in Dublin this Friday afternoon.

By late afternoon, Van is still not back to one hundred per cent in mind and body but he is determined to proceed. His intention is to make the first half of the show an acoustic set (to include some or all of the following numbers: "Madame George", "Brown Eyed Girl", "Astral Weeks", "Ballerina" and four new tunes from *Veedon Fleece*) and then after an intermission, to move into the more familiar rock section (drawing from such songs as "Ain't Nothing You Can Do", "Warm Love", "Caravan", "Into the Mystic", "I Believe to My Soul", "Here Comes the Night", "Come Running", "Moondance", "Domino", "Caledonia", "Sweet Dreams Of You", "Listen to the Lion", "Gloria" and others).

It was obvious from the opening that Van's illness was still plaguing him. He went straight into "Astral Weeks" after fairly polite applause but had trouble getting it all together. He retired from the stage after the first number and returned a few minutes later while the band filled in with a funky instrumental. Van somehow struggled through an hour's performance, but it would have been unfair in such circumstances to impose critical judgment. He did the best he could and although the set lacked his usual fire, it was as gripping as the best of most of his contemporaries.

The often tense situation was undoubtedly not aided by the continued barrage of anguished pleas for the song "Cypress Avenue" from one very-pissed member of the audience who between numbers stumbled down to the edge of the orchestra pit and shouted his requests. Far from comfortable, Van was applying non-alcoholic resuscitation at the end of each number and the last thing he needed was a loudmouth screaming requests at the top of a well-developed set of Belfast lungs not six feet distant. If looks could stun, the inebriate would have been carried off on a stretcher. As it was, Morrison's road crew warranted commendation for not freaking out and disposing of said gentleman by rapid and forceful means.

"Cypress Avenue . . . please Mr. Morrison . . . sing Cypress Avenue . . . pleeeeeeease . . . . man you've *got* to sing Cypress Avenue . . . please please pleeeeease." Christalmighty!

Strolling about the theatre between shows, one is astounded by the scores of empty liquor and wine bottles scattered between the seats. Yet the usual sweet herbal aroma of grass is notable by its absence here. On close examination the late show crowd are also laden down with bottles and as the people start filing into the theatre, the three bars are soon brimming. The majority clutch their drinks as they return to their seats several minutes after the bell clangs.

The acoustic set, understandably, has been dropped from the second show and the Caledonia Soul Express lay down a powerful thirty-minute jazz-oriented set, well worthy of favourable mention. Their repertoire covers unlikely sources: McCoy Tyner's "Song for the New World", Freddie Hubbard's "Straight Life" and two remarkable originals by drummer Dahaud Shaar, "Funky Hinkle" and "Orbital Transport". It's real jet-age jazz, whistling along on a cushion of imaginative soloist interplay, and the audience responds warmly.

The band members warrant individual attention. Drummer Shaar, of Armenian extraction (and his wife, Jean, who has been handling the sound mixing tonight) has been with Van for four years. The Shaars were discovered by Van in Woodstock where they had operated a small recording studio in the days when Morrison was a fellow resident.

Bass player David Hayes, the youngest member of the Express, was previously with Jesse Colin Young's group and joined Van in 1972. Six months ago Van secured the services of guitarist Ralph Wash (who'd spent three years with the Paul Butterfield Band) who replaced long-time Morrison guitarist John Platania, and keyboards man James Trumbo. Trumbo was highly recommended by Van's arranger of several years' standing Jeff Labes and by Stephen Pillster, who had once heard him play in a "scratch band in a garage". Van was also impressed by a tape of Trumbo he'd heard and so Pillster tracked him down to an organic food store where he was employed.

The most recent addition to the Express is horn player James L. Rothermel Jr. who is a well-known San Francisco musician with previous experience in the Jesse Colin Young band.

It's no secret that Van had been keen for many months to get Rothermel into his band and when you hear him play, it's easy to understand Morrison's admiration. Really this dude could almost blow up a squall singlehandedly. The whole band, in fact, is made up of thoroughly experienced and talented musicians and they represent real potential to become one of the foremost innovative combinations in the history of this music. You catch glimmers of it already – when they cook, it's a real banquet and there ain't nothing left on the back burner. It's all out front, sizzling with incredibly inventive solos. There seem to be no passengers on this particular Express.

Van's second set of the night is more relaxed than the opener but you don't need to take the Hippocratic oath to appreciate that the man is still suffering from the lingering aftermath of the 'flu. Again critical appraisal does not seem in order. The audience can dig it too – there appears to be this understanding that the man is just doing his best and it's pretty damn good by Dublin standards. The encore "Gloria" gets everybody off their asses and they roar for more. Wisely Van decides to pack it in for the evening and seek further rest.

Sitting in a silent stream of dreams in a cab outside the backstage door after the late concert, we four are drawn into a weird rap with a member of the audience who wants to score a Van Morrison European tour T-shirt. He hitched down from Belfast earlier in the evening and he seems in no hurry to return. We ask him for his impressions of the concert. "Shit," he says in a tone of surprise, "I didn't come here to *enjoy* Van Morrison – I came to criticize him. You've got to understand it man . . . I live just around the corner from Cypress Avenue in Belfast and I still live there and that should tell you why I came here. I don't want to enjoy Van Morrison . . . I hate him. Tell me, you must know the guy, why didn't he sing 'Cypress Avenue'? Where's his head at not to to do something like that? Why won't he play up in Belfast?

"Anyway man, come on and give me that T-shirt. You bastards are off around the world tomorrow. You can get more shirts. I'm stuck here in fucking Ireland."

The vibe is rather heavy and his words keep buzzing in our heads. Geoff Brown, the scribe from *Melody Maker*, will use the incident to lead off his report on these Dublin gigs.

Van and the band are staying in a converted manor house hotel on a bluff overlooking Dublin Bay, the setting utilized for the jacket of *Veedon Fleece*. It's a long, uninspiring thirty minutes later after a spirited rap with the cab driver who is earnestly informing us of the remoteness of the Belfast fury down here in Dublin. "We may be only a hundred miles from fucking Belfast but it might as well be a thousand miles," he says. "Those people are crazy up there. There's nothing like that down here. When you try to get a job in Belfast, the first thing they want to know is what your religion is. Down here we don't care about things like that. We'd just as rather they got rid of the fucking lot of them up there for all the good they're doing. Those cunts in Belfast are maniacs. All they can think about is their fucking religion. I suppose it's alright to have a religion but there doesn't seem much point in killing other bastards for it."

"Yeah, well they certainly seem a bit weird," jokes Stephen Pillster, sitting next to the driver. "I can't count how many of them came up to me tonight, demanding to know why Van wasn't playing in Belfast, his home town. They've got to be crazy. I don't think Van or any of us can relate to what's going on up there."

Conversation lulls as we contemplate bloody visions of religious warfare to the north, and then pass a scrawled schoolyard wall graffiti near a light pole asking: "Why Free the Price Sisters?" "Someday," muses Pillster, "I think Van would like to go into Belfast and play a couple of weeks at the Maritime Hotel. But obviously not until the people get themselves straightened out up there." Nor at the Maritime Hotel, which has since been converted into a clubhouse for the British Sailors' Society.

Eventually we pull through the manor gates and into the gravelled forecourt of the hotel. We find Van and the band relaxing in a high-ceilinged, wood-panelled drawing room, tucking away drinks and sandwiches in the lap of a huge carved wood fireplace. There isn't a lot of idle chat and Van and his lady soon retire with a quiet exit. Hardly a word is uttered by anyone about this evening's concerts. What is there to say?

"We're all kind of spaced out behind the Irish gigs," Pillster explains on Saturday afternoon. "We hadn't played for two weeks and it's not easy to just jump right back in where you left off. It hurts Van like a knife through his heart to do a show that is not absolutely top notch by his own standards. But I think it'll be fine tonight. Van's been getting some rest and he sure needs it. I just can't imagine why Van would want to come back here. It ain't so wonderful here [in Dublin] and if it's worse up there, Christ . . . I suppose Van is the one in five million who got away from it."

The long-haired gent from Warner Brothers dared to question Pillster about the possibility of interviews. "I don't think so man. He's sleeping now and there's a wedding party about to start right below this room so I don't know what going to happen. I don't really think he's in the right space, with this 'flu still hanging around." There are no complaints from the pair of journalists present.

"I would have to say that Van's sole satisfaction," Pillster tells us over the phone, "is in getting off with the five other musicians on stage. Playing at a rehearsal or in the studio is one thing . . . but the focus of an audience on their music is what really gets him off. Getting into it with the other five guys is what really matters to him. The music's the thing. He doesn't give a shit about the hall or the size of the audience or feeling sick: all he cares about is playing his music."

Duly inspired we troop down for a quick, pungent Irish coffee in the Horseshoe Bar (which we have discovered in the current issue of British Airways' inflight rag, *High Life*, is regarded by the jet set as one of the great watering holes on earth) and then out into the street to explore a nearby Saturday afternoon market where tiny stalls peddle poster pictures of John F. Kennedy and paintings of the Crucifixion and assorted plastic junk. We retire to the park to peruse a *Welcome to Dublin* tourist booklet.

"Dublin", the brochure reads, "gets its name from the Gaelic Dubhlinn (Dark Pool). This is the city of Dean Swift, the savage satirist who wrote *Gulliver's Travels*, of James Joyce, the genius who invented a new style of literature (and wrote *Ulysses*), of George Bernard Shaw, Sean O'Casey, Brendan Behan and others of their stature who have made permanent impressions in the English language.

"Fox and stag hunting enthusiasts often take a winter holiday in Ireland to enjoy this sport. There are a number of hunts in the vicinity of Dublin – South County Dublin Harriers and Bray Harriers – while the Ward Union Staghounds and the 'Killing' Kildare Foxhounds are but two of the famous packs which may easily be reached for a day's hunting from your hotel in Dublin."

By the time the people start filing into the Olympia Theatre for the first of the two Saturday evening shows, I'm getting this notion that Dublin audiences really aren't quite sure what to make of their elusive Mr. Morrison. I really don't think many people are here at the Olympia to hear a concert of music. There is this strange, hard-to-define undercurrent of tension in the crowd. Perhaps it's because the majority of them are half-pissed. Some of them *look* a bit out of place too: tweed suits and ties in there with the denim and fifth-generation furs, tobacco pipes with the bottles of gin, young dudes resembling on-duty garage mechanics. Maybe it has something to do with the tradition that homecomings must invariably be an anti-climax of sorts, and even more so in the environment of a home so many of them claim to detest. Definitely there is some contribution from Morrison's own reluctance to assume any readily-identifiable artist/audience postures. Morrison is clearly not on any star trips and one suspects that the majority of this audience is expecting a star number to go down.

The Caledonia Soul Express opened the second night with another free-flowing, expansive set, music that has yet to be labelled and so the audience enjoys it for what it is. After a brief interval with the barmaids pouring in double time, Van walked on unannounced, the stage dimly lit, to polite applause. Dressed simply, as the night before, in blue denim shirt, navy blue pullover, loose dark brown trousers and brown flat-heeled boots. Already he has rejected the rock star image and the audience appears somewhat nonplussed.

During the performance, and indeed throughout all four Dublin gigs, Van said nothing to the audience other than "Thank you". No song was introduced, nor did it need to be. No glad-to-be-back-home-in-Ireland numbers. Deeper emotions are transmitted without the camouflage of words. Anyone who had listened to his records must be aware of his dedicated and uncompromising commitment to capture the spirit of his Irish adolescence. One cannot think of any artist who has caught the fleeting essence of youthful fervour quite so splendidly or compassionately.

No front-of-stage spotlights were used in any of the Dublin gigs, by Van's instruction, and there was more light sprayed on the members of the band than on their singer. The press and public had been asked not to use flash bulbs and trying to capture the evening's highlights was a nightmare. We resorted to a special Kodak film with a 1,000 ASA rating.

One must respect Van's perennial dilemma: he simply does not wish to project any image as an *entertainer*. It is I suspect his way of letting nothing get between the musicians and the audience. Without having a focal point of identification, the audience is left to face the music. And even these Dublin crowds, who seem to have come to see rather than hear, cannot resist being moved. Stripped of adornment and superfluous frills, the music becomes an unyielding power of its own. The music is the medium and the message.

Critics have been claiming recently that Van Morrison is *the* voice in seventies' rock 'n' roll and I am equally convinced. He is quite simply the most meaningful white rock/blues voice around today. One keeps falling back on that word electrifying: Van just stands there, a trifle nervous, self-consciously flicking a clutch of hair away from his eyes – closing them as the band pounds down the solos, and singing so well it damn near tears your bloody head right off. His voice is searing to the point of mental pain, like volcanic lava pelting into your ears. In white rock, it's unique; in the wider realm of the blues, I suspect that only Otis Redding and Bobby Blue Band possessed this fiery, furious quality. His voice is an expression of all the anguish and pain which daily confronts the generations brought into this weary world in the aftermath of mankind's single most abominable act, the destruction of Nagasaki and Hiroshima by atomic bombs. It is a cry of the people who no longer can fairly face the future with an air of optimism. As the writer Kurt Vonnegut shrewdly noted not long ago: "Things are going to get worse and worse and never get better again." We know it too and Van Morrison is one of a very select few able to provide solace to our tortured souls.

One does not wish to get carried away but the point should be well and truly made that when Van Morrison is on, there ain't nobody coming within a country mile of his pasture. Here tonight in Dublin, he is right spot on and it is an almost indescribable experience. Of all the white artists to have been influenced by the blues, I doubt if any person has given more in return to the form. Morrison has taken the blues and presents them in his own uniquely personal vision. With that fine band of musicians laying down those raunchy tracks behind him, Van is free to cut loose and the effect trembles upon the point of being overpowering. His own solo work on harp and sax (often in harmony with James Rothermel Jr.) is equally astounding.

They close both shows with a tastefully-textured rendition of "Caravan" and on the two occasions, the crowds go wild. The band comes back on and rips into "Gloria", with the audience bellowing the choruses as one. Ten minutes after the end of the first show, the departing people are still singing the refrain. The song captures a moment in time when we were were all much younger and the times were much simpler, and we were doing our utmost to shed our innocence.

Backstage Van and his lady are rapping to an old friend from Belfast and I accidentally overhear a few words. "It was incredible," insists the friend. "I've never seen an audience react like that in my whole life." As always Van is non-committal.

What is there to say? Humility hangs heavily in the nicotine-tinged air.

The second show is an even bigger audience sensation than the first, even despite some shoddy post-gig shenanigans which includes an empty booze bottle mysteriously projecting itself from the first balcony to the stage, some thirty feet distant as the crow flies. On the front page of next morning's *Sunday Independent*, the concert promoter is quoted: "People panicked when a bottle slipped off the balcony." Astral projection perhaps?

A roaring, standing ovation follows "Caravan" and the band returns again. Once more into "Gloria" and the audience is right in there with it. Their combined bulk almost exceeds the sound of the band. It feels like magic. At the end of "Gloria", Van leaves the stage and with barely a word departs the scene in a limousine.

The crowd, not yet satisfied (this euphoria is something akin to cocaine, one rush and there is a desperate desire for more), keeps calling for more and ten minutes later, the din has not subsided. But Van has disappeared into the dark Dublin midnight. Nobody seems to believe that anyone would want to leave behind the magic which still lingers in this old musical hall. Once again, the elusive Van Morrison has been spirited away, leaving only memories too ecstatic to be forgotten.

If the Dubliners and Belfasters who were there tonight live long enough to be grandparents, they likely will still recall the evening Van Morrison brought his music and his mystique back home to Ireland and somehow enlivened the future aspirations of everyone present.

"Down the Cypress Avenue,
With a child-like vision leaping into view,
The clicking clacking of the high-heeled shoes,
Ford and Fitzroy, Madame George."

Ten days later, after gigs in Paris, Frankfurt, Copenhagen and Amsterdam, Morrison returns to London to play a couple of nights at the Hammersmith Odeon. The performance is impressive and there are four encores and thousands of people pouring back in the streets singing "Gloria". Bob Woffinden of the *New Musical Express* observed: "The band played with absolute competence and not a little artistry (that horn player was quite brilliant) and Morrison sang with reserved, diffident professional polish."

Morrison returned home to California and it seemed that at long last, his performing career was in high gear. Stephen Pillster passed along the information that Van couldn't have been happier. Why, he'd even gone as far out of line as to attend the closing night party of the tour. Pillster declared. Could we really believe that this mysterious man had finally emerged from self-exile?

Three months later the news whistled across the Atlantic that Van had ceased working, at least temporarily, with the five members of the Caledonia Soul Express. "There's nothing that says we have parted company," Van insisted at the Montreux Festival in July 1974 where he appeared with a specially-arranged three piece group comprising Dallas Taylor on drums, bass player Jerome Rinson and Pete Wingfield on keyboards.

"I'm not working with the Caledonia Soul Express this week or this month but there's nothing that says we parted company. We just don't know. They don't and I don't. Right now they're trying to get a couple of sets together of mainly jazz stuff and their own original numbers. And right now I'm experimenting with other things. Who's to say if we're going to play together again or not. Nobody knows at this point. I have no definite plans. None of us know. Time will see what develops."

Quite clearly Van was going through some changes as far as his performances were concerned. His set at the Montreux Jazz Festival, his first without the Caledonia Soul Express, included only two familiar tunes – "Street Choir" and the Lenny Welsh R & B standard, "Since I Fell For You" – plus eight new titles. A few members of the audience were disgruntled by the omission of Morrison songs that they knew and loved, and were notably vocal in their reaction. Backstage Van's road manager of the past three years, Ed Fletcher commented: "They can't expect him to keep on singing Domino for the rest of his life." It was a valid point. His new songs were outstanding, regardless.

The next day I asked Van if he had made a decision to drop all his older repertoire from future live performances. "I don't think anything is the be all and end all. In certain periods you other times when I was really on and I got the audience off. They do one thing, and in certain other periods, you do another thing. I don't know what's happening. I'm just the same as everybody else . . . I don't have a clue what's going on. Sometimes it's good and sometimes it's not. Sometimes it doesn't bother me in the least doing all that old stuff, and other times it does bother me. And vice versa. It all depends on how it feels . . . When it gets to the point where you're doing it all the time. I think that what I'm looking for is a happy medium."

Van has come to view himself as an existential performer. "It's a generally accepted fact that people can only see something if it's stuck right in front of them. That's the way it is in show business and the music business. In order to be a musician in this business you have to assume that show business thing too and that's where the existential thing comes in, the illusion of it all. First of all you're a musician but once you step out on that stage and once you're going to give those people what they want, that's when the illusion takes over and that's when you become a performer.

"The thing with me is that I am definitely not a programmed performer. I can only perform when I feel like I want to perform and it's coming out of me. It's hard for me to just push a button and start performing. I guess it's easy for a lot of people but not for me. I don't suppose that many people in the music business even think in those terms . . . that performing is existential. They just can't see it.

"Audiences don't see it through you. It's not in front of them. They don't want the mirror happening. They don't really come to look at themselves. But really that is what's happening. So if you happen to be not on . . . you can take it to the point when you turn your back on the audience and that's cool. There's nothing wrong with that. That's just as crazy as them coming to see you. It's really all the same trip. It's absurd really. Because they're coming out to see you when they really just want to see themselves. That's what I mean by existentialism.

"I suppose some people might think that I don't give a shit about the audience but the opposite is true. I think I care too much about what the audience thinks. During the past year or so, I've pleased a lot of audiences and when it gets to the point where I've pleased a lot of audiences and the time comes for me to be myself and maybe I don't please just one audience, that's the one they always talk about. They don't talk about the only talk about when I didn't get them off. It's human nature I guess." He pauses thoughtfully.

"To me, the music industry has got about as much meaning as a comic book. Because if I turn around and have a million-selling album or a couple of hit singles tomorrow, then the industry is going to love me to death. I'm gonna be like great . . . they'll think about all this money I'm going to bring in for them. Except that if this same cat turns around and has a couple of off nights – then they think that the cat's off, he's weird, he has off nights. He's this and that and the other thing. I can't live like that. Either I dig somebody or I don't. I can't dig somebody because they've got a hit record or they don't. That's not where I'm at."

14 Whatever the medium, the message is the same: The media

There's this ancient and wizened show business tradition regarding the way the creative soul is supposed to handle a critical media: don't give a hoot what they're saying about you just as long as they're still spelling your name right. On reflection this attitude would appear to require, even demand, a particularly callous and insensitive soul to maintain lengthy allegiance to the theory, especially if one was in the target zone of a chronically hostile press. With the laser-like penetration of hindsight, might I humbly suggest that the entire tradition sounds typical of the sort of low line that the merchandizers of art manufactured in an asinine attempt to placate the tender sensibilities of those whose task was to create the product. Example. A Hollywood actor complains to the studio mogul because his wife is annoyed by gossip mag. stories that he is balling every beach bunny in Santa Monica. "Don't worry," soothes the bigwig. "At least they haven't forgotten about you and you're still pulling the suckers in at the box office. And tell your wife that she wouldn't have that mink or that diamond necklace if it wasn't for those schmucks in the press." The box office was all that mattered.

Very few people from any profession can honestly claim to be immune to prolonged media opposition and critical outbursts: and this surely must be especially true in the case of those poor souls entrusted with the creative bent. Rock-hard shells are simply not the nature of the beast . . . it is intensely vulnerable to shots and pokes from all sides. One obviously needs a truly sturdy soul to battle ever onwards optimistically, face against a barrage of publicly-disseminated putdowns (in the press, radio, TV, magazines etc.), particularly if such criticism is rarely constructive.

There is, I believe, an inherent chink in the armour of every creative warrior for the simple reason that the act of creation seems to simultaneously produce a quite vicious variety of vulnerability, unknown one would imagine to accountants, train drivers or furnace stokers. This all the more so if the creative individual is also endowed with an inexhaustible pursuit of perfection, a condition which appears to haunt most of those who genuinely aspire to any notable degree of expertise or originality in this craft of creation. On one hand, it's hard to disagree with Matthew Arnold, who observed in the last century that "the pursuit of perfection then, is the pursuit of sweetness and light." That it well may be, but the bitter truth still remains that the perfectionist is all too overwhelmingly aware of his or her personal limitations, both real and presumed. His or her life, accordingly, is plagued by a closed curtain of uncertainty.

It is difficult enough to exist as a perfectionist in the toils of everyday industry and profession, where success and failure and their innumerable variations can at some point be starkly and conclusively worked out on the bottom line of a balance sheet. Art and creative endeavour possess no such convenient guidelines or referees. Failure in one term (say sales or popularity) can be success in another (brilliant originality) and vice versa. Only a work's creator can make the judgement, and this is where the media can exercise a sinister role. The only real success is immortality and of that, nobody on earth can ever be positive. The doubts drag on.

Liberace may have conveniently coined the phrase that he "laughed all the way to the bank" about hostile reviews, but who's to know for sure that he has not shed a bitter tear or two over the years at the some of the hysterical slams he has been accorded by music critics? The eighteenth-century writer William Cowper once described the press as "Thou God of our idolatry" but that was a much more religious age and he neglected to mention that God help our poor idols for what they will consistently receive from the press.

In the rock music field, most of the musicians and composers exhibit what might be loosely termed a love/hate relationship with members of the media. To be more specific, I think it could be fairly said that there is a lot more hate than love: certainly respect for the media by rock musicians is notable only by its absence. For several years the industry masters convinced the musicians that it was necessary to maintain an air of friendliness in company with the media, but in recent times, it would appear that the majority of artists are only concerned with tightening up the so-called "one-to-one" relationship they desire to create with their audiences. To the new breed, the media is virtually superfluous, some outside third party pushing to cut itself in on the existing action.

For its part, the media desperately hankers to forge for itself a position as the sole and definite arbitrator of what is good or bad, and which music is due the public's enthusiastic support. This has proven to be a wholly fruitless task. In our time, we have seen Top 40 type radio wither and die as the artistic adjudicator of rock music. And we have seen many, many superstars rise to the mountain top with barely a favourable word from the media, and more likely, many words to the contrary. One feels compelled to draw your attention, once again, to a 1,900-year-old quote from the Roman emperor Marcus Aurelius which appears in the introduction to this book. Nonetheless the media has a job to do in the context of rock music and that, I presume, is to inform the public about what its favourite artists eat, drink and wear (in the case of some publications) or what they feel, buy or attend (as befits the consciousness of the owners and/or editors). At the present time, the media would not seem to wave a very potent wand in guiding what the public should buy in records or concert tickets. A score of good reviews will not necessarily make a new album a best-seller just as a hundred bad reviews will not prevent an LP hitting number one. There is no shortage of testimonials to either contention. I would not go as far as to accuse the rock media of impotency but the track record is quite mediocre. Nowadays a successful rock artist can make it with or without the media's support and in some ways, that is a healthy situation from the creative viewpoint.

Van Morrison, the subject at hand, is one musical artist who makes absolutely no secret of his disdain for the media, and more precisely, for its current function in his area of artistic activity. That in itself is by no means an unusual outlook in the contemporary rock scene, but Morrison's reasons for this attitude emerge as unique under further examination. Unlike many of rock's top stars, who are convinced that they have somehow in their success incurred the wrath of the gods as manifested in the media's insurgent slashes into their respective egos (and indeed few of us could deny the typical rock critic's worship of obscurity for its own sake, and his disgust at mass acceptance which is not an inherently evil occurrence in all cases) – after all, how can anybody have the cheek to put down the aesthetic levels of a concert where 20,000 people rose from their seats and roared at the end, even if a bare one-tenth of them were able to detect in the acoustics of a sports stadium anything beyond a static roar of sound: the box office remains as the industry's bible – Van Morrison's discord with the media has virtually nothing to do with its evaluation of his musical merit. Many top rock recording and performing artists are thoroughly pissed-off at the media for something not much more substantial than a string of less-than-ecstatic album and gig reviews. They figure that if an LP is capable of selling in excess of one million copies then it is beyond criticism. It is once again a regurgitation of the merchant philosophy of quantity over quality.

On the other hand, Morrison appears to suffer from what one is tempted to term an excessively-adoring press. He has very little sympathy for certain contemporaries who spend their careers moaning about what the media is doing to their music and their egos and unable to perceive that it is the total structure with which they are at odds, not merely the isolated rip-off review of an album or concert. One imagines that Morrison is confounded by the rock scene's broad lack of perception in this context.

Morrison does have a reasonably clear idea of just what he personally dislikes about the media *en masse*. He professes to detest misquoting of his comments, absurd assumptions about either his art or his person, poorly-researched interviews, misrepresentation of his music and his manner, plain lies and horseshit, and the inevitable reappearance of old, off-the-cuff comments presented as the definitive truth. In a phrase, Van Morrison loathes lack of professionalism. It's not hard to believe that he also finds little of a commendable nature in the rock media's overall evaluation of the music scene, its strange desire to drop a match in a dry box and be the first to scream "Fire", and above all else, its lack of critical dissection of the music industry in total. In this final aspect, Van probably suffers from a degree of naïveté: it would appear that the last place where you'd expect to find the critical torch being turned on the music industry is within the music media, being as it is almost completely dependent on the same industry for advertising support. The conflict of interest looms menacingly.

We working rock journalists like to assume that there is a certain professionalism meandering through the craft. It's doubtful if many us us would claim that the level of professionalism is riding at an all-time high in the annals of writing, but nonetheless, it's still pleasant to bask in the assumption that a certain code of decorum and ethics does exist. We who diligently strive towards, at the very least, accuracy, honesty and sincerity, simply cannot believe that some journalists would have the audacity to alter, to suit their own ends, the words of others. Surely if there is a single ethic in the journalism field, it must relate specifically to being accurate when representing the expressions of other people, whatever our opinion of them might be. We who mightily declare that it is *our* traditional right to pass judgement on the creative efforts of others would do well not to overlook *everyone's* right to saying what he or she thinks. This equality cannot be over-emphasized. Yet if we are to accept what involved participants like Van Morrison and many others are telling us, there is a woeful lack of professionalism at work in the rock media.

Morrison clearly feels that he has been done formidable misservice by certain elements of the media. He claims that he has been regularly misquoted, misrepresented and almost invariably, misunderstood. In the course of the past few months, I have pored over hundreds of thousands of words written about Morrison and I must reluctantly admit that his claims are justified. You'll find several examples within the outside quotations utilized in these pages.

In the summer of 1973, Van and the then general manager of Caledonia Productions, Inc. Stephen Pillster, put their heads together and ultimately decided to take a positive step towards rectifying the situation of inaccuracy. They hit upon a novel concept: the publication by Caledonia of a seventy-two-page reference press book on Morrison entitled, a trifle slyly, *Reliable Sources*. In the introduction it was noted: "For him [Van], what is written about his music is not as real as the experience of the music. He accepts that nothing written about him will be perfect. Caledonia Productions has produced this book to get out information that is as 'true' as possible. The music, of course, is its own statement."

As source material, this publication is the most comprehensive and professional effort that I've had the pleasure of perusing in a decade of the morning mail piled high with innumerable, puffed-up bullshit stories about recording artists. As duly noted elsewhere, *Reliable Sources* has been a constant companion and valuable reference in the spadework required to write a book such as this. Instead of merely complaining about the state of the media, Morrison took steps to alleviate some of the basic problems and he is to be heartily commended for it.

"I think I just basically wanted to show how ridiculous the journalists were and the press in general. I don't know if I accomplished that . . . I think I'd like to do a better one sometime. Most journalists are kind of like managers in many ways. They want things to happen instantly and if they don't happen instantly, and if they don't get the right story they want, then they become upset. But rather than admit it, they go and write something bad about somebody. They take it out on the wrong people. I don't know . . . if they take themselves seriously, then they really do have a problem. It's really not that important. They make it more important than it really is."

Before delving into Van's own comments about distressing experiences with the rock media, it would be appropriate to quote from the "Words Without Music: Interviews" section of *Reliable Sources*, to size up the Caledonian viewpoint. It says flatly:

> "Van doesn't enjoy being interviewed. Aside from the fact that he changes his mind just like everybody else (and words appearing in print have a tendency to stabilize the artist in a pose which may not be typical of him), he gets angry when he sees fact blown into fantasy in articles about him.
>
> "For example, an article in a European newspaper stated as a fact that at one time there were twenty groups claiming the name 'Them'. It went on to say that there were four Them's simultaneously gigging in the United States. Granted there was a controversy over the use of the name Them, but there were at most two or three groups Them at any one time. Not twenty. In another article covering the Them period, a writer said that Van used to read from the Bible on stage. It wasn't a Bible, it was a book of poetry. Recently Van was described drinking beer with a writer. Van stopped drinking a few years ago. This sort of innaccuracy makes the media lose credibility in Van's eyes. He does his gig as well as he can. He expects the same from others."

As well he might.

When Van was holidaying in Ireland in the autumn of 1973, a writer for the *New Spotlight* magazine asked him it it was true that he didn't like giving interviews. "I have had some bad experiences," was his frank reply. "I've been quoted out of context, quoted wrongly and most of the articles are innaccurate. They seem to be into sensationalism and the danger is that a lot of people take it as gospel."

Morrison had never been one to fraternize with the media in general, but in 1971, after a series of allegedly fantasized quotes, he decided to withdraw as much as possible from partaking in interviews. He just could not justify the damage that assorted inaccuracies could conceivably drop in the way of the public's relationship with his music. "People would just call up asking for interviews and I'd tell my manager I didn't want to do any," Van told *Sounds* writer Steve Peacock in the spring of 1974. "I guess I just didn't feel like it . . . I didn't think I had much to tell anybody. I did, I guess, but I just wasn't into it and I remembered all the times before when a lot of rubbish was put out. So I thought: 'Why bother?'

"People just assume that you're part of a scene or this or that – that's what's wrong. I definitely don't fit into what's happening in the music business. Most of the people in that scene, whether they're writers or whatever, they tend to think it's weird that I'm not coming in and telling everyone how great I am and how great my records are and what my new suit's like. They think you're weird because you don't do that, just because everybody else is doing it . . . hyping their records, hyping themselves. I really don't care what these people think, I'm just concerned with getting to my audience. I care about what my audience thinks. But if people are going to tell my audience things that aren't true: I don't need that.

"People make up stuff about me, about anyone. The sick part of it is that people believe it. Many people fall for what they see in black and white and if they see something in print, then they'll go for it. People have been putting stuff out on me since I was with Them and maybe five per cent of it has something to do with me, but the other ninety-five per cent doesn't. What do you need that for? I'm just not a rock star. I'm just a singer. I don't know what a rock star is. I think the only people who know are the people who write about it, because they're the ones who are putting it out. Most of the artists themselves are just doing their gig, just doing a job."

Rather convincing evidence of what Van terms the press's "thriving on myth" revealed itself at a 1973 press conference in Amsterdam, Van's first in more than six years. *New Musical Express* writer, Roy Carr, himself no stranger to the intimacies of the scene, was appalled that Morrison could walk through the centre of his own press conference twice within five minutes and remain totally unrecognized. There seems to be a shortage of people who are genuinely drawn to the scene through love of the music or admiration for the people that create it. There is this speckled periphery which has little to do with music or art or anything other than hanging around.

Bearing this superfluous scene in mind, it comes as no surprize that Van occasionally throws a harmless if somewhat cynical spanner into the media works. After *Rolling Stone* interviewer Happy Traum observed that "Madame George" appeared to be the story of a drag queen, Van claimed that he saw it as a "Swiss cheese sandwich". Tired of being mercilessly hounded by questions about what his songs really meant, Morrison has been known to urge a writer that his understanding might be well-served by simply listening again to the lyrics of "Domino", from the *Street Choir* album. "It wasn't a significant statement," he subsequently admitted. "I might well have told him to go and read the sports results. It was just an expression. People read things into them that weren't there. I once told someone in a joke that I fly around the room and again it was made into something."

It is no revelation that Morrison has a particular disgust for the mediocrity of Top 40 format radio, and the entire obsession-with-singles attitude which continues to pervade the music industry. "It definitely hasn't changed much," he said recently. "But that's the way they make it. I know a really great singer who's with a certain record company, she is a coloured chick and she really is a dynamite singer. She told me 'I'm waiting for a hit single'. 'What's the point of going on the road if you don't have a hit single?' she said. I think that's ridiculous. If a record company has got a good artist and they know the artist is good – that is, that they can sing and they are good at their art – then either the company should get behind them or they shouldn't sign them at all. Why sign somebody and have them sitting around until they get a hit single?

"But this thing has developed over the years. People have been thinking 'We've got to get a hit single before we do this or that.'

I really don't know why they keep singles going because it seems such an old thing. It used to be that when singles were selling and all the radio stations played were singles . . . but then it changed. It's very weird.

"I think of it as a joke. I thought for a while that it was changing. I remember that in 1967 something really seemed to be happening with the radio stations and all that, it was starting to get to be really good. All of a sudden it just turned around again. People had been starting to get into playing what they wanted to play; and then all of a sudden, click, right back into another trip again. It didn't last very long. All that shouting coming at you. I've got to admit that I was very lucky in the singles aspect because Warner Brothers never forced me into that. There is one radio station, KTIM in San Rafael out on the West Coast that is pretty good.

"Another thing is that the music magazines contribute very much to it. The well-aimed music magazines, the ones that know what they're doing and who know what they're selling, just keep cranking the rubbish out and people are buying it."

What irks Morrison the most I suspect is the manner in which the media allows fact to degenerate into fancy, and the way some interviewers have tried to intrude their own personalities upon the sacred soil of his music. He feels that too many writers get carried away by their own illusions: they seem almost to be possessed by the subjective. It does appear that much of the published material on Morrison has only served to get in the way of the music. "I just feel like it's their little fantasy trip," he once said. "It doesn't have anything to do with me. It's like the public are digging your art, whatever your art is."

Much of the fantasizing and imaginary explanation can be attributed to the near-worship status accorded him by people, press and otherwise, who have been converted to his music. Some individuals are so profoundly moved by his music that they feel entitled to make undue assumptions about its creator (which in itself is the traditional fate of all artistic souls). Irrelevance becomes the order of the way. I keep recalling the time when Californian rock writer, Danny Holloway, journeyed to Marin County to interview Van and prefaced the publication of the transcript with the comments: "After all this time of listening to his records and memorizing every word, after all those long years of adulation – I didn't even like the guy."

I fail to see how it matters. Journalists appear to shoulder a belief that their personal reactions to Morrison in the tight confines of a brief interview will somehow provide their readers with a greater understanding of the man's music. How?

Even the hallowed pages of *Rolling Stone* (a magazine which, to its credit, has long been a keen booster of Morrison's music) have come in for Van's criticism. In June 1972, *Stone* published a long, loping and notably sympathetic profile of Morrison in which the writer, John Grissim Jr. allegedly "made up" a dream-inspired explanation of the *Saint Dominic's Preview* title song. Van quite angrily informed *Zig Zag*'s John Tobler that: ". . . he [the writer] gave me his word that he was going to print it [the interview] exactly word-for-word off the tape, and when it came out, it was all changed around."

Over the years, Van Morrison has gained what appears to me to be an unfair and unsubstantiated image as a super-tough interviewee, an artist who has the nerve (read balls) to say what he thinks, how he thinks and why he thinks, sometimes to the detriment of those present. Ask a stupid question etc. Granted that the man is a perfectionist, a soul whose music means an immense amount to him, and that he really despises a lack of professionalism. If he has demonstrated some cynicism in regard to the media, it is only through a series of unfortunate experiences which have annoyed and perplexed him. He can find no justification for such hassles.

I believe he cares deeply and passionately about the state of the music scene and its media, not only as it involves his own career but also as it applies to the forest of young hopefuls who aspire to recording and performing success as rock artists. The current scene frustrates him enormously, all the more so because there seems to be so little that he can do about it. "It's really such a flash in the pan," he observed recently. "How can anyone get a dozen new records and review them in the same day? It really does a lot of harm (to an artist) if you get a reviewer who really isn't that good. What happens if it's somebody's first album and the reviewer happens to be brought down that day and he writes a review that completely slams the album? That's probably going to kill that artist for a long time.

"It goes back to that old thing: I don't know what it is but it seems like that they (the media) never want you to be what you are. If you're not doing well, they want you to do better; and if you're doing pretty well, they don't want you . . . but they never want you to be where you are, they always want you to be somewhere else. They act like there's something wrong with success. You make records because you want people to enjoy them, that's what it's all about.

"I think I can see how this thing works. There are so many acts that aren't very good, but are very successful. So I can understand how the public can see someone on the box and think: 'I can do as well as that.' I can see that kind of thinking. It's frustrating. I'm an artist myself and I'm frustrated. I'm frustrated when I see a lot of so-called superstars playing what I think is rubbish. And I know people who are really good and they're not getting the breaks for one simple reason: not because they're no good, but because they don't have a name. Nobody knows their name and that's why they don't get a break. You have to get about forty million people running around saying somebody's name before it can get out in front of a good audience.

"So few people are into the music; for most it's the scene and that's the hit. It's happening in England and it's happening in America. People are into making the scene. Who's got the flashiest shoes? How big a fad can this be this week? My jacket's from this place, and your pants are from that other place. It's all down to fashion or something. I don't see how it's got anything to do with music. I can dig it for what it is but I wouldn't go to watch it myself. I don't pay money to go and see what somebody's wearing. I want to hear what they sing and play, not what they're wearing. It's very hard for me, because there's definitely too much emphasis on the wrong things. I just don't know . . . it's all screwed up. Let's face it. What can you say but that it's all screwed up?"

And so Van Morrison continues eluding them. Just as they think they've got him pinned down to a frozen stance, a tree on which they can nail a label, some cute little trite phrase, he's up and off again. They call him the "Marlon Brando of Rock", "the missing link between Ray Charles and Bob Dylan" (which seems to me more a case of Dylan being the missing link between Ray Charles and Van Morrison), the "Belfast Cowboy", but none of it means a thing to him. He absolutely shuns it. The artistic force is ever-changing, ever-moving, ever-revolving. Like life itself, it never ceases for a moment. Motion defies effective categorization.

"The only reason journalists call me a myth or a legend," he told Roy Carr in 1973, "is simply because they can't think of anything else to write. It's a convenient label. A name is a product. If the music is good, it's really not all that important who's playing it. Names are secondary. I'm just a vehicle for the music to come through. I'd honestly prefer people just to call me a musician and leave it at that, without being portrayed. But you don't do that kind of thing in this business. Not if you want to make a living."

Morrison won't even subscribe to various theories that he is a cult figure in the rock scene. "People have told me that I have this cult following, but I don't think that's true at all. It's really just people who have been hanging in with me for a long time."

Van just won't squeeze himself into the pigeonholes. The music is all that matters. It really *is* as simple as that, a fact that very few members of the media seem able to grasp. Perhaps they never will understand. And so, in more lucid encounters, Van has conceded that the entire myth-making, media image trip – the press kits, the photographs, the interviews, the articles, the music magazines, Top 40 radio, the wild misconceptions – all of it means just one thing to him and the word is "bullshit".

15 If this is music, it might just as well be jeans or baked beans: The music industry at large

Most raw young recording artists, when first confronted with the inner mechanism of the music industry (that sprawling monolith whose sole function is to process art into an assembly-line production, transforming lovingly-created studio tapes into something that befits a supermarket rack) tend to be horrified at the relative unimportance of the actual music in the merchandising machine. But as time glides by, egos are appeased and as the coffer doors open to reveal outrageous rewards, early dismay gradually changes to well-insulated acceptance. A few recruits, more sensitive to hypocrisy than their colleagues, continue to voice an artistic protest at the product orientation they are forced to endure. You're a number not a name, young man. In the main however, such expressions of dissension are by far outweighed by the dull drone of silence emanating from the majority of successful artists. Silence is golden, in more ways than one.

As a consequence only a handful of musicians and composers, strange people who put their art way ahead of the money, have the guts to perennially resist the mediocrity and moronity which is wildly rumoured to infect the music industry. Van Morrison has those kind of balls. For the past decade, he has fought a notably bitter battle against what he feels is an abominable and indeed, inexcusable status quo. His career is a remarkable example of the lengths to which an artist has to go to maintain purity in his art. It may well be an authentic history of the music industry's greatest-grossing years. Where it was *really* at.

It is hardly surprising therefore that Van Morrison should prove to be distinctly volatile in discussions of the music versus product dilemma of the recording/performing artist. He especially resents the laudation of the personal manager's role in the rock industry, he has few kind words for the breed. To his mind, a manager should be an extension of the artist's desires and aspirations; rather than some blundering unmusical fool who issues perverse instructions on what his artist should wear, how he should live, what he should sing and how he should answer media interrogations. You see, Van Morrison is his own man – this being a character trait which has brought a measure of grief to several managers in the past. His soul cannot be bought and sold. He remains unimpressed by how much extra loot he might acquire by doing something his manager's way: he knows what he personally wants and financial rewards generally bear little influence on his career direction. Such an unyielding, un-American outlook would not appear compatible with the sort of manager whose vision is restricted to the projected gross for each concert and album – and I don't need to tell you that the music industry is overloaded with that type of individual.

Van is committed to an inner belief that he should not compromise his art and, of course, he dreads being relegated to a position of mere product in the channels of music industry commerce. He steadfastly insists that he is an artist, a composer, a musician, a person . . . but never a product. "This word product keeps coming up," he said a couple of years back. "If I'm the product, then these people (managers) are supposed to be an extention of how I operate. If they're not, they are operating against me. And that's what happens to a lot of artists. It's part of an older generation setup that has nothing to do with this generation. There's a brand new world now . . . our generation. I want to do it the right way, here and now. I don't want to live by anyone's old philosophies."

What he is implying is that the old school – ageing executives who control most of the music industry, motivated by profit regardless of aesthetic cost – is just not where he's at, and that he is no happier about the countless wolves in sheep's clothing, the long-haired, cocaine-snorting, hip young guys who erect a veil of compassion for artistic endeavour when they too are solely concerned with how much money they can stuff into their pockets. The laws of libel prevent us from adopting a more specific approach.

In Van's eyes, the music industry suffers from a predominance of ignorant types who are moved by names and money and have next to no awareness of the music as music. "I think most of the problem stems from being fly by night," he once observed. "A dee jay is fly by night, rock 'n' roll is fly by night. It's all fly by night stuff. There's nothing really solid there.

So people do something for a year and then all of a sudden, they've gone somewhere else or are doing some other trip. Like a fad. And fads don't go anywhere. I think it works if people are into what they're doing. If someone's in the music business and doesn't really know music, they shouldn't be into it." (This last remark concerned radio station programme directors who exercise indirect control of many aspects of the industry.)

As regards radio programmers, what really bothers Morrison is the lack of musical diversity and restrictions in free-form innovation by idiotic categorization. "For me there's not enough Hank Crawford, David Newman and people like that. I think the reason that they don't get into a wider market is because people have categorized it. People have categorized jazz like they categorized rock 'n' roll. I think it's just mainly lack of education . . . or the dee jays on their part. I mean the people who aren't really into their gig. They don't really have the education. They play what records come out. 'Well so-and-so's got an album out this week', so they play that. But there may be six other good albums out that week that they don't even think about because nobody's saying the other names. It's like that trip with the king's new clothes. They catch on or something.

"It seems like all the music has got caught up like selling jeans. I mean, if they don't know . . . if they don't have ears: then it never gets on the air at all. I don't think the music business is really the music business. I think it's another kind of business and they're using money as a front or something, like public relations or something like that. It's not music. It's all down to the names thing, it's just down to names and images . . . it doesn't matter how good you are at doing your gig, that's got nothing to do with it. It's just politics or something."

In November 1973, on being asked why he was not an ardent enthusiast of the way the music business works, he replied: "Let me put it this way: there are those artists who love it because that's what they're into, just making the scene. A lot of them don't seem to have any voice at the back of their heads. Maybe it's because I'm a Virgo or something but I just think there's more to it. I just think the music industry, from the situations I've been through and what people I know have been through, is just ridiculous. Most of it is just totally ridiculous.

"I'm in a situation now where I'm lucky, so it's not ridiculous for me anymore. It's good for me. I'm doing what I want to do most of the time now, and as far as my record company is concerned. I'm not saying that they're fabulous guys. They're just people. I don't complain about that. I think I'm having it really good now compared to some people who have been eaten up by it. You just can't let that happen; that's basically what I'm against. People being sucked in by the whole trip.

"My record company and I have disagreements, there's no doubt about that. I figure they should be doing more of this and that. But I don't think there's enough artists helping other artists . . . to make people aware of what's happening and that it's not just a free for all. You've really got to think it out and all that stuff and one of the few people who is doing that is Frank Zappa. I think Frank Zappa is a very intelligent human being. I think he's got a lot to say. He's about the only artist I've heard of really saying things in interviews. He says things about how it works, what you shouldn't let happen and what he thinks should happen. I think it's really good that he's been outspoken like that.

"I'd like to hear more people who are really successful telling it like it really is, instead of pretending about it. It's the old take-the-money-and-run principle. I find that the music means so little in the music industry. I really do find that, and it's amazing when you find it all over the place. People seem to get to a certain point and then they're not into the music anymore . . . they're just into gimmicks or something."

The names of Messrs. Jagger and Bowie were introduced with due reverence and Van commented after a slight pause: "I just can't figure them out . . . maybe they're genuine, God, who knows? I don't know if they're genuine or not. I always think they've got talent these people, but . . ."

Finding himself at odds with most facets of the merchandizing of music, Van Morrison has instituted as many barriers as possible to insulate and isolate himself from the industry in recent years. With the formation in 1971 of his own company, Caledonia Productions, Inc. he began to assume piece by piece the all-important creative control of his own music which he implicitly believes, with reason, is a personal right. Caledonia Productions was organized for the expressed purpose of giving him "artistic freedom and control over his music", a noble objective one must agree. In the past, such control invariably had seemed to wind up in outside hands, to the detriment of Morrison's career. If it wasn't a staff producer from a record company, it was somebody in the art department or a transient personal manager or a booking agency employee.

Prior to the full flourishing of Caledonia Productions, Van had a string of managers including Bert Berns, Schwaid/Merenstein and Mary Martin. Although he does not offer any personal putdowns of these individuals, it is abundantly clear that their achievements suffer in comparison with the progress of Caledonia Productions. It was rare for Van's intentions to coincide with those of his manager, for whatever reason.

A few words on the subject of the Caledonia name might be in order at this point. By now you must have noticed that Van Morrison seems to be obsessed with the word: he's used it to name his production company, his studio, his publishing company (Caledonia Soul Music), and his backing groups, the Caledonia Soul Orchestra and the Caledonia Soul Express. He frequently adlibs the word in the closing refrains of his songs and in the spring of 1974, he recorded the old Woody Herman/Louis Jordan swing standard, Caledonia.

Caledonia is reputedly an ancient land which was once part of what is now called Scotland. It has not appeared in maps since the time of the Roman invasion of Britain; Caledonia was one of the few areas never actually conquered by the Romans which indicates extremely stout powers of resistance. Very little is certain about its history but it is quite obvious that the mystic nature of Caledonia has inspired a legion of "mad" Irish poets over the centuries.

Van Morrison sincerely believes he is a Caledonian, at least in spirit. When he first toured Scotland, he claimed to have discovered a "certain quality of soul" with which he felt an immediate empathy. He subsequently discovered several years after he first began composing music that some of his songs lent themselves to a unique major modal scale (without sevenths): which of course is the same scale as that used by bagpipe players and in Old Irish and Scottish folk music. Van suspects there may be some connection between soul music and Caledonia. Certainly his own music has almost indefinable tendencies in the direction of a strange feeling which transcends the gamut of everyday rock 'n' roll endeavour. Whether it is linked, in some romantic way, with Caledonia is an eminently debatable topic. What really matters is that Van believes he has "the spirit of

Caledonia in his soul and his music reflects it". Who would doubt that it provides valid inspiration?

In the summer of 1973, Morrison hired a young man named Stephen L. Pillster to act as general manager of Caledonian Productions, an arrangement which was to last almost twelve months before they parted company. Pillster, an affable, seemingly-sensitive Californian, functioned in broad terms as the go-between for Van and the outside world and music industry. He was frequently referred to in print as Morrison's manager but it would have been more correct to regard him as Van's envoy or representative. Not that such fine distinctions imply, even for a second, anything derogatory about Pillster's activities. He was not employed by Van to be a yes man or to hang around soothing the artistic ego. Far from it. While Van did the writing, recording and performing, Pillster pulled the various arrangements together.

The initial conception, I gather, was that Pillster would take care of Van's business activities, lifting a considerable burden off Morrison's shoulders and allowing him to concentrate all of his energies on creating and making music. Caledonia Productions, Inc. was Van's own production company, but it required a trustworthy and together individual to oversee the day-to-day activities. In return, Pillster was to receive a weeky salary plus expenses, but he was not contracted to a percentage share of Morrison's gross, as in the normal management relationship. It seemed to be just the type of arrangement that would suit Van's purposes, and it was something of a shock when Pillster departed, although it must be said that the latter always made it clear that their relationship might be a transitory affair. He did seem prepared for just about any eventuality.

Pillster spoke candidly and sincerely about the role he played in Van Morrison's organization: "I had previously managed Dan Hicks and his Hot Licks, but when I first met Van through a friend, Steve Cowan, I had been thinking about getting out of the music business. I'd considered going into real estate or opening a restaurant or something. I love the music business but it's a love/hate relationship. I'd been a fan of Van's since *Astral Weeks* and at the first meeting, we just seemed to hit it off. I talked to him and found out what was needed and we tried to establish a situation that had been lacking in the past.

"What we were trying to do was set up a situation which

The latest Warner Brothers' publicity shot

Ritchie Yorke

In Montreux, June 1974

Live at the Rainbow Theatre in London, autumn 1973

Van and daughter Shana on the Rainbow stage in London, 1973

Trevor Humphries

would stand, no matter what. If Van was to decide tomorrow that we couldn't get along together anymore, then someone else could come in and pick up the reins. It was a matter of getting his organization together. I felt that Van had needed somebody in that position for a long time. Too many people in the past had been into a trip of 'what can we get him to do that will make some bread?' . . . there was far too little appreciation of his artistic sensibilities.

"While Van is a musician, he's also a poet . . . or at least a combination of both. Unfortunately I think the standard of contemporary musicians is just smoking, snorting, fucking and sucking. Van is not there at all in that trip. His band was aware of it and they could dig it. . . . He deserves to be treated as a poet."

One of the first tasks which Van assigned to Pillster was the production of the *Reliable Sources* media guide. "When Van and I were first talking, we had a long conversation about various things," said Pillster. "One of the things which really distressed him was the misrepresentation and misquotation in the press. So I asked him who put all the background information together and he said he thought it was Warner Brothers records. I suggested that we might spend a few dollars to establish a reliable source for all media people. We called it *Reliable Sources* and the thing just grew and grew.

"Originally it was to be only sixteen pages but we found so many good things to use. The actual book, I think, gives a good accounting of Van over a lot of years. I feel it amply demonstrates that he's an artist with real durability. It also came in a three-ring folder which means it could be expanded on at a later date. Of course I can't deny that the editing of it was subjective." Still, as *Reliable Sources* rightly mentioned in the introduction to the record review section: "Van has had very few bad reviews."

Pillster indicated during his association with Morrison a commendable desire to alleviate grass-roots business hassles and, I suspect, demonstrated to Van that he indeed could function efficiently without the usual personal manager situation. One is inclined to doubt if Morrison will ever return to that type of arrangement. As he pointed out three years ago: "I feel I'm not the type of artist who can have a manager. So right there that puts the music business through quite a few changes. It means they have to deal with somebody who's not a puppet, who doesn't function like a clockwork robot. I'm a human being, not some kind of wind-up doll."

As far as Pillster's departure from Caledonia was concerned, Van observed: "He just stopped doing what I wanted. When it started out, he *was* doing what I wanted. He was working for me, but it ended up he wasn't working for me. So we just couldn't go any further. He just wasn't doing what I wanted done. Maybe he was sincere at the beginning. Who knows? It was just one of those things, it just didn't work out."

As for the future of Caledonia Productions, Van appears to be reconciling himself to the fact that he may not be able to find somebody to handle the running of the company the way he wants it run. "I don't think anybody can run my business, but myself. Because I'm the only one who knows what I want. Everybody else seems to want to make millions. They want to make it tomorrow . . . they want to make it really fast. They want to be really successful in a short period of time and they really get immature about it.

"I've been in the record business for eleven years. I didn't just arrive on the scene. I don't need to go back in time, but unfortunately most of the business people you meet just want to keep on going back and doing all the things they haven't done that I *have* already done. The only way I think it could work with me is if I got a cat who'd been through similar changes to what I've been through. Then it might be alright."

As far back as the summer of 1973, Morrison felt that he wished to expand his creative efforts beyond his own work. He wanted to become involved with assistance and encouragement of other artists, both new and semi-established people, this in spite of a couple of less-than-satisfying experiences as a producer for other record companies. His first such venture was the writing and production of four songs with Jackie DeShannon for Atlantic Records, the singer who had contributed backing vocals to "Warm Love" and "Hard Nose the Highway". The arrangement was more in the line of a return favour. He later admitted: "I don't really dig producing people. I can't see myself fitting into that category. It's a dangerous game."

Van also produced some sides with the veteran blues singer

guitarist, John Lee Hooker, a man who has always rated Morrison very highly. The sessions did not seem to produce much artistic reward, for Van commented to the British rock writer, Roy Carr: "I've experimented with producing other artists, but I've come to the conclusion that, when you really get down to it, it's not really worth the effort. It's not really yours. And it's a really hard gig because you hardly get anything out of it. I'm not talking about the bread, I'm talking about artistic satisfaction."

With the expansion of Caledonia Productions, he had a different trip in mind. He claimed that he wanted to "conserve music, not just produce artists, because that starts getting like you're producing an artist to make something like a hit record and that's not really what I want to do." One of the first steps was the installation of a 16-track recording studio in the grounds of his former Fairfax, California home. At one point, he envisaged it becoming a commercially-operational set-up, available for hire to other members of the industry. But that soon changed. "It got all weird with about twenty cars in the driveway and people lying all over the ground stoned and stuff. So I didn't do that again."

The Caledonia Studios have brought Van further creative freedom, but he feels there is still something lacking. "It's good," he says, "but there still isn't complete freedom because guys like engineers have to come out from the city and you can't have them standing around for days at a time." Van will not commit himself to any technical aspirations in operating the recording board himself, but he's accumulating information in this area. "I know how to turn the board on and off and I know what all the knobs and sliders are for but I have an engineer who operates all the machines." Both the *Hard Nose the Highway* and *Veedon Fleece* albums were recorded at the Caledonia Studios, and Van claims to enjoy the fact that he now produces his own records. "It's a lot harder work and sometimes when you're stuck in the middle of it, you can't see the wood for the trees. But it is rewarding."

Van has pointed out that he wants to "put out other types of music I'm into and people I play with are into. I'm sort of like a jazz artist where the jazz artist goes in and cuts an album and they put it out. That's where I want to get to . . . he walks into the studio, he blows and then he comes out."

The enlarged artistic scope afforded Van by Caledonia Productions has sparked off other possibilities. He plans to complete a book of poetry in the near future. "I'm always writing. If it's not songs, it's poetry or prose. It's hard to draw the line between songs and poetry; some of my songs are poems. 'Madame George' for example. The whole thing just needs editing."

Above all, Caledonia is providing Van with a well-earned opportunity to direct his career on all fronts. He has even managed to secure control over what appears on his album jackets. "I'm just realizing the impact of record covers," he said recently. "I didn't think that people read so much into covers. Especially if they don't have any information at all – they just look at the cover and they just make things up about what's happening."

And so the man who has always believed that the artist who creates the music should have some right to decide how it is presented to his public, has finally worked his way up into a position to do just that. All of the bitter clashes of yesterday – the confrontations with record companies and production companies over unauthorized albums, the conflicts with publishers over lack of royalty statements and payments on his copyrights, the stupid decisions by managers representing his art, the tremendous difficulty in maintaining any degree of personal integrity in the web of an industry which does not appear to care what the word means – have become the events of other times. Van Morrison survived the rigours of a jungle to prove that it could be done; he has shown what an alienated artist must do to preserve real honesty in his art and he's done it in a manner that many of his contemporaries would be wise to speculate upon.

In the final analysis, it seems that he took on the modus operandi of an indecent industry and won. "The music business hasn't really changed all that much," Van told Roy Carr of the *New Musical Express* in 1973. "They're still draining the thing dry. The same people are still in charge. They're just a little updated. I've found out that success is not what the magazines or the industry says. It's up to the individual to say what success means. For some it's being the biggest thing at any particular time and drawing the biggest crowds.

"I dig success for what you can do to help other people and that you can demand artistic freedom . . . that is of course if you want it. The only trouble is you have to plough through all the shit to get where you want to be. I guess I've been one of the lucky ones – in spite of everything. Really it was kind of like winning the football pools."

16 Some observations on the most sacred subject of all: His music

Unlike so many of his contemporaries, willing slaves to a merchant culture which has next to nothing to do with art, his music is all that really matters to Van Morrison. Such a phrase may have lost some of its potency in times when it has been bandied around with reckless abandon by literally hundreds of hypocrites. "My music is all that matters, man" is a line we've all seen on more occasions than is comfortable to recall, especially when the claim has so often proved to be counterfeit, the cry of the wolf. Many have laid claim to the hypothesis of art above all else, while being more concerned with how much bread they can bulldoze into their bank vaults, how much cocaine they can imbibe into their de-snotted nostrils, and how many times they can make it with a gregarious groupie, all in the course of an evening. As a former close associate of Van's, Stephen Pillster, candidly observed in a previous chapter: "Unfortunately the standard of contemporary musicians is smoking, snorting, fucking and sucking." 'Tis sad but true.

Yet so many superstar musicians resort to ridiculous means to convince their audiences of the sincerity of their intentions, although it so rarely rings true. Ask not for whom the bell tolls. The majority of them continue to view success as the top of the best-selling charts and six-figure nightly concert grosses, without any genuine consideration of the value of their music. It is extremely uncommon for a musician to admit that despite massive success in industry terms, his music leaves a lot to be desired. Merchant-musicians tend to count success by the ring of the cash register, not by the quality of the product.

Humility, like humanity, is an unusual asset in big-time rock circles. Stars aren't made to such proportions. They may start out with these attributes, but the nature of the industry is all but guaranteed to smother them. It's a brash, brisk and bitter pursuit, this lust for rock stardom. I'm almost tempted to suggest that it brings out the worst in people. The rock quest frequently reminds one of a shark attack: once the beasts sense the smell of blood (read money) in their frozen nostrils, they begin to tremble either from excitement or a nervous twitch, and then charge in smashing up against each other in the rush for the flesh. It is a far from attractive sight. But, as the Romans were fond of noting, Art has no enemy except ignorance.

The last bastion of the American Dream it has been called. The sole surviving marketplace where anything goes, capitalism unlimited, souls for sale, the only place left where fortunes can still quite literally be carved out of rock overnight. So much lovely green treasury paper lying loose in denim pockets. So they created idols to draw out the idle cash. The product swivels off the shelves just as fast as they can shove it out there. In out, in out, the fast buck on its merry way. Get on the phone man, we gotta get more goods. Now. And we wanna special discount. We'll take a thousand pieces of the product. Don't ask me where we'll store it – we'll shoot it straight up on the shelves. Be gone by tomorra night. Get rid of that blues shit. Move it down the back racks. Ya gotta sell to be on those display shelves. Product that moves fast, that's what counts. The rest is ratshit.

And they invented nice, meaningful names to describe their scene. Rock and roll. The dance of life. Teenage delight. Fabulous. Fantastic. Outasite. Gas. Groovy. Great. Unbelievable. Unreal. Incredible. You know man. The industry of human happiness. The business of love peace joy hope salvation heart soul heaven. Gettin' da folks off. Raising consciousness. Catching the evening tide and riding it around the world, knights at night upon white swans. Careering into dawn. The fate of the Brave New World. The merchants of artistic invention.

But how *good* is it? Who gives a shit? If it sells it must be good. Anything else is irrelevant, you schmuck. Musical quality? Christ, who can waste precious time bothering with such trifles? Even if they possessed the capacities to arrive at such pudgments. Get down to where it's really at: product playlists plant-capacity phonographs photographs press-kits accountants lawyers contracts pressings tape-rights T-shirts sales-incentives freebie-goods re-orders rack-jobbers record-months re-signing review-copies catalogue-numbers units-moved. Dig the chant of the unholy. Now what's that about art? Whattayamean, integrity?

Damn it man, Van Morrison is *so* determinably different. He doesn't fit the picture. Their game isn't his game. Not any more, now that he's learnt how they played with his music. Now he knows that he can reject it and them. He doesn't consciously conspire to produce catchy little pop songs to appease the feeble minds of many who programme Top-40-type radio stations (not to mention record companies); he doesn't turn out at boozy receptions to suck up to bloated members of the media; he doesn't sign concert contracts unless he's satisfied that every member of the audience will be able to share in the intimacy of his music, which of course rules out sports stadiums and arenas; he doesn't employ a publicist to tell people how fantastic he is; he doesn't want to assume any static, fixed, easy-to-relate-to image; he doesn't wish to be regarded as a product or a catalogue-number; he doesn't demand that foreign licensees of his records supply him with dope and pills when he's on tour; and he doesn't allow anyone to push him out onto that road which leads to rock stardom and its Pandora's Box of paltry acquisitions.

I really cannot believe that he cares all that much about how many records he sells. It's a pleasant feeling to reach a high chart position (and presumably to enlarge the audience for one's music) but to Morrison, there are more important aspects of the musical endeavour. He simply desires to get the music out to the best of his ability and that is a factor which has very little connection with *Billboard*'s weekly best-selling charts, regardless of the industry's contentions.

His music is all that matters and it really is staggering that so many fools have vainly attempted to prevent him from making it the way he wants to. The fact that he has won while they lost does not excuse the damage they have tried to do. The intent overrides all.

Yet as close to his heart and soul as his music obviously is, it continues to be a subject on which he has very little desire to elaborate through the processes of the media. He would appear to hold fast to this conviction that the music simply is, and one should make of it what one can. No appraisal of his music is of any relevance, he feels, because the conclusions must be inherently subjective. Each of us finds in his music what we bring to it, and if a particular song might remind you of a treehouse in Oklahoma and your friend of a duckpond in Glasgow, then so be it. Enjoy it as you can. It is not conceit which brings Morrison to this conclusion: it is merely the sum total of the media's imaginative response.

Comparisions with other artists are equally odious to both Morrison and his more dedicated enthusiasts. Van's music and his approach to his art are so unique that to draw parallels with other singer/songwriters is absurd. How does one compare a rose with a narcissus, a tomato with a pumpkin, marihuana with tobacco? The futility of grandstand observation is all too obvious. Some people have compared the work of Dylan and Morrison which strikes me as being an exercise in idiocy. Save the trees. Paper is too precious. Much more effective to get out on the field and listen to what the player has to say about himself and his style, and about what he personally admires in other music.

Of his eight Warner Brothers' albums up to and including *Veedon Fleece*, Van considers "Madame George" to be his finest single track and the one which he enjoys the most. "Definitely 'Madame George', definitely. I'm just starting to realize it more and more. It just seems to get at you . . . it just lays right in there, that whole track. The vocals and the instruments and the whole thing. I like that one."

Somewhat sheepishly one asks him if he hopes to create something of similar ilk in the future. "I think that it will be different. I mean, I dig the whole *Astral Weeks* album. It's really hard to pick just one track off it. For me it all pulls together. If I came close, it would be in a different way . . . it would be like another trip."

It does come as a distinct surprise to learn that of his extended works and the short punchy tunes, he prefers the latter. "The way I see it, you can break it down into two things: there's the part that's for the basic audience, then there's the stuff that you're personally really into. I prefer the shorter stuff myself."

He does not claim to completely understand the creative motivation in some of his material, although I think he has been remarkably lucid in explaining many of his songs in these pages. "Sometimes the songs are finished right after you've written them, period," he once said. "I'm sure there are people at university sitting around trying to figure out what James Joyce meant on page 23 of some book he wrote, but I'm not into that. Somebody will be trying to figure out what Robbie Burns meant when he said blah-blah-blah. It's whatever it means to *you*. That's all there is. If there's anything beyond that, then it's in your head and you're taking it from there."

Van does not deny the pervasive influence of adolescence on his lyrics. "Definitely some of my songs are influenced by my childhood in Belfast. But I don't think my music has necessarily changed from sad to happy. In all kinds of music, you can't have just one thing. There's happy music and sad music and in between music. I don't like to be categorized. I like to do a lot of different things."

He claims not to suffer from a shortage of new song material and in the spring of 1974, he said: "I'm just writing like a madman. I do so much I'm caught: I've got old stuff that I haven't put out yet. Some of it is already recorded, some of it hasn't been. I've got some stuff that I didn't write but I have recorded and that hasn't come out yet. Then I've got new stuff that I'm writing. I guess I'll know what's next when it comes out. I'd like to try and get some of that old stuff out sometime, but I just don't know where it's going to fit in. The longer you wait, the harder it gets. You're working on new stuff and the older songs get further and further away. One tends to be more excited about the newer things.

"Yet some things that you do seem like now all the time. When I play live I get much more into that. You can do a song like forty times and it could still be new. Others songs you can do twice and you don't dig them anymore. I don't know what it is but sometimes that's how it works out. I'm writing songs to entertain people. If I write something, it's not necessarily how I'm going to feel in a year or tomorrow. It's a total thing . . . a flow."

As a brief diversion, it's interesting to examine some of the comments on Morrison by other recording artists. Says Gregg Allman, himself one of the most tasteful musicians in rock: "Van Morrison is one person who has never made a song that I didn't like." John Lee Hooker notes: "He's my favourite white blues singer . . . and one of the greatest around." Bob Dylan has admitted that he "likes the way Van Morrison sings". Adds Dave Mason: "There's no one to compare his voice to. It's unique. That, together with the overall effect of his band and his arrangements, makes you feel so good, so alive."

"Van is a great blues singer," in the words of Jackie DeShannon, "one of the rare few who can drag you through the most down lyrics, really make you feel them, yet at the same time bring you up." Taj Mahal says. "I love his ideas and the way he approaches his music. He lives it, he puts the feeling on you, and that's where it all starts from."

Van himself is not particularly impressed by the general standards of contemporary rock music and he does not bother to hide the fact. When he's at home, he prefers to listen to blues and jazz albums. "I like people like Mose Allison and Gil Evans," he says. "But I don't like heavy rock 'n' roll . . . it doesn't turn me on. I don't like screaming guitars and stuff like that. I'd rather listen to Carl Perkins or Chuck Berry for rock 'n' roll.

"I did think Art Garfunkel's solo album [which includes a Van Morrison tune, 'I Shall Sing', also cut by Miriam Makeba] was great. I thought Roy Halee did a great job on production. Art just came up to the studio one day and asked to hear some of my songs. As soon as he heard 'I Shall Sing', he said 'That's the one'. My arranger at that time, Jack Schroer, arranged it for him. I wrote and recorded the song in 1971. I've got a lot of stuff in the can.

"And of course I dig the Chess label material too. I think David Newman, the sax player, is a great soloist. Dig him doing 'Lonely Avenue' sometime. I like The Band . . . I always look forward to their new albums." The Band are among an extremely elite handful of artists with whom Van has been agreeable to sharing his creative spirit. Van first met the group when they were recording their second album in Los Angeles in 1970. When he returned to his home in Woodstock, he renewed the acquaintance and one afternoon a jam session took place. They played for about four hours and he and Robbie Robertson wrote a song called '4% Pantomime' (the title relates to the spirits proof in alcohol) for The Band's *Cahoots* album.

"I wrote most of the lyrics and part of the music," says Van, "and Robbie wrote some of the lyrics and the rest of the music." Van later said he would have liked more time to work on the song: it was rushed, he said, because he had to fly right back to Los Angeles. Van was a guest singer on the sessions with Richard Manuel. He maintains that he does not know the members of The Band intimately.

The only rock album that Van claims to have purchased in recent times is Traffic's *Low Spark of High-Heeled Boys*. "I heard it on the radio a few times and I dug the title track [which, perhaps not coincidentally, concerns itself with the uglier aspects of the music industry] so I picked the album up. I like a couple of cuts. I'm not really a rock record buyer. I buy more jazz records."

Attending rock concerts (other than his own) is also an infrequent exercise. "I don't go now at all," he said in November 1973. "There's really nothing I want to see. I don't really think people are saying much as far as rock 'n' roll goes. To me Chuck Berry was saying more than anybody is today. It's really hard to admit that but it's true." He made an exception early in 1974 to attend the Bob Dylan gig in San Francisco, but walked out halfway through the concert. He refused to comment further.

His own best-selling albums (in order of unit sales, as reported by Warner Brothers in June 1974) are: *Tupelo Honey, Moondance, It's Too Late to Stop Now, His Band and the Street Choir, Saint Dominic's Preview, Hard Nose the Highway* and *Astral Weeks*. One makes no comment.

In an attempt to gain some further knowledge of what music most moves him, I asked Van to name his five all-time most treasured albums and after due reflection, he replied: "I'd definitely include *The Best of Ray Charles*. There's just something about that album . . . I really love it. It's all instrumental tracks and it features David Newman on sax. I have an album of Renaissance vocal music which is German I think. It's very quiet so I'd pick that. I'd definitely include *Astral Weeks*. Then there's an album by Shakey Jake called *Shakey's Blues*, on the Prestige label. And I'd include another of my own albums, *Veedon Fleece*. That's it."

From a lesser talent, the inclusion of two of his own albums in such a short list might appear impertinent. But in Morrison's case this seems perfectly reasonable. Who wouldn't include *Astral Weeks*, for example, in any compilation of great albums? Van Morrison's gift is a remarkable one and I suspect he knows it, albeit in a totally unegotistical context. When he ventures his opinion that "Madame George" is one of the finest pieces of music the past two decades have produced, it is merely because he has come to realize what the song has been doing to so many heads. It has nothing to do with conceit. His music, he says, is simply "in me, and it's just got to come out".

As for visions of his future, he hopes to be in a position to continue making records indefinitely, spending as much time as is necessary to put it together to his satisfaction. "When a record happens," he notes, "the record company turns around and says give us another album. A lot of people just walk in and do another album without going through working out the thing the way it should be done. I think you need some kind of workshop. I think it's just like acting – if you just walk in to a part it's not going to happen the same way as if you'd been in a woodshed working on it."

But what about this heavily-lauded spontaneity trip, sitting around in a studio until the songs somehow tumble into place, the way in which the Stones are supposed to work? "I think it's probably a good idea for the way *they* write. They're into a certain momentum when they write. But when you get some time between you and the song, you're looking at it from different angles."

For all the production controls that have been wrapped around his music in the past, Morrison has never been one to spend a lot of time fooling around in the recording studio. "He has a sense of black and white about all things to do with his music," says Stephen Pillster, "When he's in the studio, he'll usually do a couple of vocal takes and if it doesn't come together, he moves onto something else. He's not into overdubbing at all." Ted Templeman, Warner Brothers' staff producer who has worked with Van in various studio capacities, has said: "He works fast and demands the same of everyone there. I've had to change engineers who couldn't keep up with him. He hates to do re-takes on vocals."

Van has long nurtured a desire to cut a country and western-oriented album. *Tupelo Honey* started out with that concept but never quite came through. "I've definitely got a country and western album planned," he says. "It will have songs like 'Wild Side of Life', 'Crying Time', 'Banks of the Ohio' and stuff like that." One of these years, he's going to release a Christmas album. "We tried to do one in 1972 but we were under too much pressure. You have to start making a Christmas album on January 1 if you want to get it out in time. We'll probably do some originals and a few of the old things like 'White Christmas' and 'Chestnuts Roasting On An Open Fire'. All that romantic stuff."

There was also the possibility, according to Stephen Pillster, of a concert and album with the Denver Symphony Orchestra. "Van is open to all sorts of different forms with his music," Pillster told me in the spring of 1974. The man himself seemed far less positive on that score.

"I'm not going to do a gig with the Denver Symphony," he said emphatically. "I'm not into proving it. There's a million things that I could do, but what for? Why do you do something? Because you get off. But I don't think it would mean anything for me to do something with the Denver Symphony. It would just mean that another rock singer did something with a symphony orchestra. The general consensus is still that I'm a rock singer. So it wouldn't mean anything. In any case, I've already done concerts and an album with strings. It wouldn't make any impact.

"You see, it's hard for me to do all that stuff. All these people come into the picture out of nowhere – all those hundreds of people show up and want to get involved. They only show up when you do something . . . if you're not doing anything, they don't show up. I'm just at the point where I don't want to deal with those people. And if it means that I only do one tour a year, then that's what I'm gonna do because I just don't want to see those people. I don't have to see those people and I don't have to deal with them.

"So if it means I do less in my career – if I fall short in some of my artistic spheres – then that's what will happen. I just don't want to get involved with all those business people. It would be nice to do all those things but I don't want to see those people because they're just creeps . . . I mean, they're really creeps. I think it's a pity of course but that's the way the business is. So I'm going to do one tour a year and the rest of the year I'm going to write and record. There's supposed to be an album every six months but it never seems to happen that way. I don't know what goes wrong and I have no control of it. *Veedon Fleece* was finished in the spring yet it won't come out until the autumn. I wish I had more control over things like release dates. Now, at least, I do have control over the music and the jackets. I'd like to also get control of the release dates of my records. It takes so long to get them out sometimes that I really can't believe it.

"I'd just like to keep on making records," Van concluded in November 1973 summing it all up. "If I can do that, it will be great for me. If I can just keep doing that. I don't know . . . I think it all works. If you can see farther than today or tomorrow, if you can see farther than that, then you're doing great. That's what I think. I'm taking it as it comes but I still know basically what the plan is and if I get the chance to do it, I'm going to be happy. Just like I'm happy now."

17 "If they want to know anymore, fuck 'em!": Personal life and future

"I believe that an artist does not belong to the public but to himself. I don't want anyone to know anything about my personal life because it is my personal life to do with what I wish, like anyone else. When a working man comes home on Friday night, what he does Saturday and Sunday is nobody's business but his own."

(The Van Morrison Archives)

Still they keep on asking: what's he really like? Where's he really at? What gets him off? What dope is he into? What does he do at home? Van Morrison's enthusiasts have this insatiable curiosity about the man's private life and what he's into off stage. The fact that he projects no familiar image on the stage seems to make the urge to know more about the real person even more acute.

This obsession with Van's personal life probably has more than a little to do with the everpresent nostalgic stimulus of his music and lyrics. He has managed in an unrivalled manner to rekindle the passions of our childhood, the simple earnest joys which possessed us before our eyes were opened to the disintegration through plunder and greed of the world around us. Captured in our innocence, as it were. If Bob Dylan at one time expressed some of our growing alienation, Van Morrison recreates a gateway into a bed of splendid childhood memories. As Thomas Gray observed a couple of hundred years ago: "Where once my careless childhood stray'd, A stranger yet to pain!" The joyful times before the pain began, before we uncovered the truth. And faced the proximity of our fate.

His love songs, of which each album has been liberally sprinkled, are earnest and universal. Who will not admit to some personal association with "Crazy Love"? Or with "Brown Eyed Girl"? Or "The Way Young Lovers Do" or "Moondance" or "These Dreams of You"? Or even "Listen to the

Lion"? One just can't deny it because truth will stand. Van Morrison has indeed provided us with an escape into another, infinitely more beautiful space. He is the link to personal memories which have lain dormant for a decade or more. He opens the door to beauty and grace, two of the most sorely-missing elements in this turgid technological age. One is inclined to believe that we'll still bask in the memories invoked by "And It Stoned Me", "Wild Children", Cypress Avenue", "Come Running", "County Fair" and other songs long after our own children have grown up and taken wing. Morrison's music, as much as anything else produced by rock artists during the past twenty years, has durability. It frequently appears to this ear that his music becomes even more powerful with age.

The consistent brilliance and eminence of his music has been a major contributing factor, I think, to this preoccupation with trying to pin down just what the man undergoes and is influenced by in producing it. Wary as he is of baring his soul to the media at any time ("He is normally suspicious of people who do interviews" Stephen Pillster once wrote to me), Morrison is even more cagey and cautious when it comes to discussing his personal life. Usually he won't even allow the subject to be broached by interviewers. He goes out of his way to discourage questions which touch on what he does when he's not in the recording studio or concert hall. If some writer does get a shot through his defence, he will provide an unsatisfactory answer or draw his working man's Saturday–Sunday analogy.

In 1974 he told *Sounds*' interviewer Steve Peacock: "I think my personal life is really none of their business. I can't speak for other people. I don't know what it's like to be a super star and have people follow you around wanting to know all about your life . . . but I do think it's nobody's business but mine what I do with my life. If they dig my music great but I don't relate to this any differently than if I was a clerk. I wouldn't be telling some guy from a magazine what I did when I went home (if I was a clerk) so why should I in this business?"

Peacock bravely persisted and asked Van if, as a Ray Charles' fan, he did not have an interest in what makes the man tick? "To tell the truth, I don't," Van replied. "I've dug Ray Charles for a long time but I don't give a shit about his personal life. I identify with what he's saying. But I'm also realistic enough to know that if he says something on a record in 1955, he's not going to think the same in 1974."

Van's life and his art are completely separate spheres, he steadfastly claims, and he professes amazement that anybody should think differently. Media's answer to that of course is that in becoming a recording artist and performer, a public personality so to speak, then one must invariably be faced with a consuming public interest in one's total life. They say it's a professional hazard of all show business but Van ain't having any of that jive.

His privacy is a precious personal possession and one not to be taken lightly. It should be preserved at all costs. But it's an old feud of the creative artist and one that is seldom won. Obviously Morrison does not pack up after a gig and go home and forget about music. It's his whole life; it does not turn on and off like an auto. The drum is always beating. And not being satisfied with the music industry's status (low) quo, the trip is seldom far from his mind.

Naturally when he's at home, he likes to be away from the scene where he works. Put another way, his home is not within the circumference of the rock scene. It is not a social centre for music industry hangers-on and hoi polloi. The rock jet set don't scream their wheels in his backyard. In the words of one of his best-known anti-stardom lines: "I don't want to spend the rest of my life changing my phone number every thirty days." To protect himself from an invasion of hasslers and hustlers, he has put up a veil of secrecy. He does not want to be bothered. If there's something you want to know, check in with his office. But human nature being what it is, this elusiveness is a catalyst to even keener curiosity about him. Christ, he might even be hiding something to indulge in such fierce protection of his privacy. Why else would he go to such lengths to avoid what to many rock artists is the ultimate success achievement: a reception for the media in the domestic setting.

The truth is that Van Morrison leads a notably quiet and subdued life and he has very few consuming interests other than music and simply being. This does not imply that he has shut himself off from the world; merely that much of what is going on out there either infuriates or is of little interest to him. When he first moved to the United States in 1967, he based himself in Cambridge, the university town near Boston. Business forced him to move to an apartment in New York. None too comfortable with the big city environment, he moved to Woodstock in upstate New York a few months later. It was a sympathetic creative atmosphere. "Everything was cool because there were a lot of musicians around who understood what being a musician meant and they left us alone when we wanted to be. This was before Woodstock happened. We used to play at Slade Hill Café . . . played there just jamming with a group called the Montgomerys and we did a few gigs around there. It was the sort of place to go when you came off the road. It's not a happening place really." The Band were also Woodstock residents during part of this period although Van was not on intimate terms with the five members.

In 1968 Van married Janet Planet, a comely dark-haired lady he'd met one night after a Them gig at San Francisco's Fillmore West two years earlier. Ms. Planet contributed to three Van Morrison albums as a back-up vocalist. She also adorns the front cover of the *Tupelo Honey* LP. Many critics have assumed that Janet Planet was a major romantic inspiration to Van's music, but Morrison has never publicly acknowledged this. He has, however, admitted to being an ardent romantic by nature.

During their five-year marriage, Van and Janet had one child, a delightful girl named Shana (Janet also had a son, Peter, from a previous relationship). In the spring of 1971, the Morrison family moved from Woodstock across America to Marin County, just north of San Francisco. "I'd been on continuous trips to California from time to time," Van recalls, "and we'd been renting this place in Woodstock, and it just kind of happened that the lease ran out: the guy had somebody else he wanted to put into the house at that time. I didn't have another place to go and I was on the West Coast when all this went down. It kind of went down in between gigs – I was playing Vancouver, Seattle, San Francisco and up and down the West Coast, so I just looked for a house out there, rather than one back East. That's basically how I came to California.

"Also, Woodstock was getting to be such a heavy number. When I first went there, people were moving there to get away from the scene – and then Woodstock itself started being the scene. They made a movie called *Woodstock* and it wasn't even in Woodstock: it was sixty miles away. Another myth. Everybody with his uncle started showing up at the bus station, and that was the complete opposite of what it was supposed to be."

The Morrisons soon found California becoming a real home to them. Van continued to think of himself as an Irishman in some ways but home was now Marin County. "I'm definitely Irish," he said in 1972. "But I don't think I want to go back to Belfast. I don't miss it with all that prejudice around. We're all the same and I think that what's happening there is terrible. But I think I'd like to get a house in Ireland . . . I'd like to spend a few months there every year."

In 1972 Van and Janet's relationship floundered and they were divorced the following year.

July 1972 witnessed a visit from Van's parents. A few weeks prior to their arrival, he'd said: "I never had much time for my family really. I left home eleven years ago but I keep in touch now all the time." During their stay, George and Violet Morrison made the decision to emigrate to America to be closer to their only child. They arrived early in the winter of 1973 and duly opened a record store named, of course, Caledonia Records, located in Fairfax, a serene community some twenty miles north of San Francisco and near to San Rafael, base of Caledonia Productions, Inc. The Morrison parents had experience in the record retailing business in Belfast in the mid-sixties. The Fairfax store specializes in rare blues product and understandably there's no shortage of Van Morrison albums and tapes.

Morrison reads very few newspapers or magazines (none of the rock variety) and has only a flickering interest in TV and automobiles. He is getting into a lot of books, most recently the works of Jean Paul Sartre. He listens to a lot of jazz records but very few of the rock genre. He has not touched any form of alcohol for several years nor has he consumed any kind of dope since 1970. "I just got tired of doing it so I stopped. It wasn't doing anything for me any more," he says. I have no doubt that this admission will raise the hackles of numerous rock pundits who are convinced that really great music can only be created while one is under the influence of assorted stimulants.

He writes a lot, not only music but poetry and prose. He also maintains a personal journal which one fervently hopes will eventually be published as it will surely provide further insight into where the private Van Morrison is really at. He does not partake of the rock scene life, either in San Francisco or anywhere else. He shuns press receptions, including both his own, where he has been known to circulate unidentified, and those of other artists. On the road he invariably sticks to himself, usually travelling with his fiancée, and he rarely socializes, although he has been loosening up in recent months.

Even his business associate of the past twelve months, Stephen Pillster, does not claim to know him all that well: "I don't think anybody really knows him intimately . . . I certainly wouldn't claim to know him closely, but in my book, he's a genius." In essence, Van Morrison is a deeply private person. Not so much moody as sensitive and retiring. His words never spill out onto the floor in senseless heaps. It is not easy to draw him out in extended conversation, but he does at times display a wry sense of humour. He speaks an Americanized-Irish brogue, slowly and cautiously. He often pauses for reflection upon a question. He never chatters. Some would call him introverted. Certainly he's the last person one would expect to greet at one of rock's conventional post-gig group gropes, attended upon by young ladies of assorted virtue and style. He shuns the typical as if it were a potent virus.

Yet in my experience, he is a pleasant, easy-going individual. He does tend to be initially suspicious of people he has recently met, but it's important to add that he bases his opinions of them on what he sees rather than what he hears from others. His intuition appears to be a significant factor in all of his actions. In many ways, he has a warm personality, not to imply extroversion. Clothes, fashion and appearance play a minor role in his outlook. Being trendy is not his trip. He'd rather be himself.

He respects intellect and awareness and forgives lack of punctuality. Altogether I must say, if only to counteract claims to the contrary, that Van Morrison is an eminently likeable person, as well as an exquisitely-gifted artist. Many myths ride buckshot around him, but beneath the bullshit one is captivated by his honesty and sincerity. In short he's not the sort of person one often meets in the music industry.

On the odd occasion, I've even known him to loosen up and rap about his personal aspirations. "I'm getting into travelling now," he said en route back home from Ireland in November, 1973, his first vacation in several years. "I'm starting to get into travelling a lot. For travelling's sake, rather than for working. I got turned off travel because of one-nighters and all that wearing me out. But now I'm enjoying travelling for its own sake.

"I love good movies too. And I'm into nature a lot. I'm starting to get into trees and things like that. It's really weird. Some people don't seem to have the time for that." Time is what it's all about. As Van Morrison once said: "The only thing that stands up is whether you've got it or not. The only thing that counts is if you're still around. And I'm still around."

18 The Van Morrison Discography

Twingy Baby b/w Boozoo Hully Gully – the Monarchs (recorded in Germany in 1963).

THEM 1964–1966

LP *THEM* (U.S. Parrot PAS 71005; U.K. Decca LK 4700). Released 1965

Mystic Eyes	Go Home Baby
If You and I Could Be as Two	Don't Look Back
Little Girl	I Like It Like That
Just a Little Bit	I'm Gonna Dress in Black
I Gave My Love A Diamond	Bright Lights Big City
You Just Can't Win	My Little Baby
	Route 66

LP *THEM AGAIN* (U.S. Parrot PAS 71008. U.K. Decca LK 4751). Released 1966

Side One	*Side Two*
Could You Would You	Out of Sight
Something You Got	It's All Over Now Baby Blue
Call My Name	Bad or Good
Turn On Your Lovelight	How Long Baby
I Put a Spell on You	Hello Josephine
My Lonely Sad Eyes	Don't You Know
I Got a Woman	Hey Girl
	Bring 'Em On In

Them released several singles and E.P.s on the Parrot/Decca labels: Don't Start Crying Now, Baby Please Don't Go, Here Comes the Night, One More Time, Mystic Eyes, Gloria.

Decca also issued in 1970 a compilation of these two albums under the title of *The World of Them* (Decca SPA 86).

For the purposes of these recording sessions, Them consisted of Van Morrison on vocals and harmonica, guitarist Billy Harrison, Alan Henderson on bass, pianist Eric Wicksen, drummer Ronnie Millings and assorted session musicians.

BANG RECORDS 1967

LP *BLOWIN' YOUR MIND* (U.S. Bang BLPS 218; U.K. Decca HAZ 8346)

Side One
Brown Eyed Girl
He Ain't Give you None
T. B. Sheets

Side Two
Spanish Rose
Goodbye Baby (Baby Goodbye)
Ro Ro Rosey
Who Drove the Red Sports Car
Midnight Special

LP *THE BEST OF VAN MORRISON* (U.S. Bang BLPS 222; U.K. Decca HAZ 8346)

Side One
Spanish Rose
It's All Right
Send Your Mind
The Smile You Smile
The Back Room

Side Two
Brown Eyed Girl
Goodbye Baby (Baby Goodbye)
Ro Ro Rosey
He Ain't Give you None
Joe Harper Saturday Morning

Bang released the following singles: Brown Eyed Girl, Ro Ro Rosey. All tracks featured Van Morrison on vocals and session musicians. They were produced by the late Bert Berns.

WARNER BROTHERS RECORDS, 1968
(Catalogue listings and release dates refer to the U.K.)

LP *ASTRAL WEEKS* (K46024) November 1968

Side One
Astral Weeks
Beside You
Sweet Thing
Cypress Avenue

Side Two
Young Lovers Do
Madame George
Ballerina
Slim Slow Slider

LP *MOONDANCE* (K46040) February 1970

Side One
And It Stoned Me
Moondance
Crazy Love
Caravan
Into the Mystic

Side Two
Come Running
These Dreams Of You
Brand New Day
Everyone
Glad Tidings

LP *HIS BAND AND THE STREET CHOIR* (K46066) October 1970

Side One
Domino
Crazy Face
Give Me a Kiss
I've Been Working
Call Me Up In Dreamland
I'll Be Your Lover, Too

Side Two
Blue Money
Virgo Clowns
Sweet Jannie
Gypsy Queen
If I Ever Needed Someone
Street Choir

LP *TUPELO HONEY* (K46114) October 1971

Side One
Wild Night
(Straight to Your Heart) Like a Cannonball
Old Old Woodstock
Starting a New Life
You're My Woman

Side Two
Tupelo Honey
I Wanna Roo You (Scottish Derivative)
When That Evening Sun Goes Down
Moonshine Whiskey

LP *SAINT DOMINIC'S PREVIEW* (K46172) July 1972

Side One	*Side Two*
Jackie Wilson Said (I'm in Heaven When You Smile)	Saint Dominic's Preview
Gypsy	Redwood Tree
I Will Be There	Almost Independence Day
Listen To the Lion	

LP *HARD NOSE THE HIGHWAY* (K46242) July 1973

Side One	*Side Two*
Snow in San Anselmo	Green
Warm Love	Autumn Song
Hard Nose the Highway	Purple Heather
Wild Children	
The Great Deception	

LP *IT'S TOO LATE TO STOP NOW* (K86007) February 1974

Record One . . .

Side One	*Side Two*
Ain't Nothing You Can Do	I've Been Working
Warm Love	Help Me
Into the Mystic	Wild Children
These Dreams Of You	Domino
I Believe To My Soul	I Just Wanna Make Love To You

Record Two . . .

Side One	*Side Two*
Bring It On Home To	Here Comes the Night
Saint Dominic's Preview	Gloria
Take Your Hand Out Of My Pocket	Caravan
Listen to the Lion	Cypress Avenue

LP *VEEDON FLEECE*

Side One
Fair Play
Linden Arden Stole the Highlights
Who Was That Masked Man
Streets of Arklow
You Don't Pull No Punches But You Don't Push the River

Side Two
Bulbs
Cul-de-sac
Comfort You
Come Here My Love
Country Fair

SINGLES

Warner Brothers have released the following Van Morrison singles:

Crazy Love b/w Come Running March 1970
Domino b/w Sweet Jannie October 14 1970
Blue Money b/w Sweet Thing January 13 1971
Call Me Up In Dreamland b/w Street Choir April 28 1971
Wild Night b/w When That Evening Sun Goes Down September 1 1971
Tupelo Honey b/w Starting a New Life December 1 1971
Like a Cannonball b/w Old Old Woodstock March 1 1972
Jackie Wilson Said b/w You've Got the Power—July 14 1972
Redwood Tree b/w Saint Dominic's Preview September 20 1972
Warm Love b/w I Will Be There April 25 1973
Ain't Nothing You Can Do b/w Wild Children April 3 1974

Warner Brothers have also issued the special "back-to-back" singles:

Moondance b/w Crazy Love December 1971

Domino b/w Into the Mystic December 1971
Blue Money b/w Call Me Up in Dreamland December 1971
Wild Night b/w Jackie Wilson Said October 1972

Warner Brothers Music has published The Van Morrison Songbook, which includes the music and lyrics for songs from *Astral Weeks, Moondance* and *His Band and The Street Choir,* plus Brown Eyed Girl.

UNAUTHORIZED RECORDS
(The following albums were released without Van's knowledge or approval).

LP *T. B. SHEETS* (U.S. Bang BLPS 400; U.K. London HSM 5008) 1973

Side One	*Side Two*
He Ain't Give You None	T. B. Sheets
Beside You	Who Drove the Red Sports Car
It's All Right	Ro Ro Rosey
Madame George	Brown Eyed Girl

This album features Van Morrison and session musicians.

LP *THEM FEATURING VAN MORRISON* (U.S. Parrot 71053–4; U.K. Decca DPA 3001/2) 1973

Record One . . .

Side One	*Side Two*
Gloria	Mystic Eyes
I Like It Like That	If You And I Could Be as Two
One More Time	Little Girl
My Lonely Sad Eyes	Philosophy
Come On My Baby	It's All Over Now Baby Blue
Just a Little Bit	

Record Two . . .

Side One

Baby Please Don't Go
I Gave My Love a Diamond
You Just Can't Win
Could You Would You
Richard Cory
Bad or Good

Side Two

Bring 'Em On In
12 Brown Eyes
All For Myself
Half As Much
Hey Girl
Here Comes the Night

This album features Van Morrison and members of Them and miscellaneous session musicians.